Accolades for Tony Bhaur and his Writing

"Amarjit Bhaur (Tony) has been a longtime volunteer and cultural Ambassador for the work of LOROS Hospice. LOROS provides specialist end of life care across Leicester, Leicestershire and Rutland – ultimately supporting more than 2,500 people every year both within the hospice itself or out across the large geography of the 2 counties.

His calm presence coupled with many wise insights make him an ideal volunteer to spend time supporting patients and family members who need good company and reassurance as they face their final journey within the embrace of LOROS. Tony is a much loved member of our hospice community and willingly gives his time in a variety of roles, always with a smile and a deeply compassionate nature."

John Knight
Chief Executive, LOROS

"Thank you so much for sharing your book on Life, Death and After, which we both read it and found to be very useful and interesting.

Lot of effort and time is spent on research, contacts for seeking help, your personnel experiences, people's real life stories, and much more.

We think this book needs to be published as soon as you can.

 I don't know how you found time with your busy schedule to write such an intense book with so much details, which is so practical in the current situation.

 Once again thank you so much for sharing this with us."

Indra and Ashok Jethwa Yoga Teachers

"Death is often a topic of discussion that most people would rather avoid but a reality we will all face at some point in our lives; whether we lose a member of our family, a friend or pet. Life is a precious gift and this book is a thoughtful collection of heart warming stories, reflections, poems and guidance that may help the reader navigate this journey."

Kartar Singh Bring
Chair - UK Sikh Healthcare Chaplaincy Group

"I am in absolute love with how it goes from the start. It feels almost warmer and more intimate. A sensitive look into your thought process.

- I like that the lessons in grief is so concise and bullet pointed so as to be more helpful to the reader.
- I could see myself giving this to someone in their moments of need. A great TOOL for those dealing with the grief of losing someone loved and close to them.
- The question of After Death is a fear that everyone deals with and your words are a sensitive yet practical look at such a contentious subject."

Jaskirat Bains
Head Teacher Birmingham

"Thank you all for what you do for so many people!"

"Thanks for the six-tip article. I generally had a handle on the first five, but challenging the negatives (in tip 6) hit the nail on the head. The wording you use is assuring and very helpful."

"This information helped me immensely."

"The article was very explicit in outlining exactly what I was looking for. It was concise and easy to understand. And it also gave me helpful advice with the coping strategies! It is so scary whenever I've had to be the caregiver, doctor, social worker all rolled into one!"

"Very well organized and written. I just lost an incredible companion yesterday after 13 years. Thank you so much for explaining what I am feeling and for giving me permission to grieve on my own terms. This article is very much appreciated."

"You've been such a great supporter of Help Guide that I wanted to let you know the difference you've made.

We can never thank you enough for the part you've played in making this possible.

Your support has been a help to all those who count on Help Guide for safe, trustworthy, free, and easily accessible online resources!

With gratitude for allowing us to count on you as a partner in our mission."

Robert Segal
Co-Founder and CEO, Help Guide International

Life, Death And After

A self-help guide for loss, bereavement and grief.

Tony Bhaur

Michael Terence Publishing

First published in paperback by
Michael Terence Publishing in 2021
www.mtp.agency

Copyright © 2021 Tony Bhaur

Tony Bhaur has asserted the right to be identified as
the author of this work in accordance with the
Copyright, Designs and Patents Act 1988

ISBN 9781800942837

No part of this publication may be reproduced, stored
in a retrieval system, or transmitted, in any form or
by any means, electronic, mechanical, photocopying,
recording or otherwise, without the prior
permission of the publisher

Cover image
Copyright © nuttapong01
www.123rf.com

Cover design
Copyright © 2021 Michael Terence Publishing

Dedicated to...

My dear family who's been a rock of stability throughout my life.

Acknowledgements

This book has been developed over the course of many years and a huge number of people have contributed to this final publication. I am deeply thankful to Good Therapy. Org; the source of psychological explanation and expert knowledge on topics including grief, loss and bereavement. Also like to thank the following for their contributions:

- Jolyn Well-Moven
- Emily Long
- Marianne Esolen
- Kathy Hardy-Williams
- Deb Del Vecchio Scully
- Steven Pace
- Blythe C Landry
- Jade Wood
- Ivan Chan
- Dr Sidnye Ziscook
- Zawn Villines
- Katelyn Alcains
- Crystal Raypole

I am deeply thankful to the following people sharing their personal stories.

- Lemara
- Rafael Zoehler
- Lisa A Snyder

- Jennifer Martin
- Tammy Black
- Rose Stanek and Maia Delmoor

I am also thankful to my dear friends
- Mr John Knight, CEO LOROS
- Mrs Joe Kavangh, Director Care Services LOROS
- Dr K Shergill,
- Miss Jaskirat Bains
- Mr Balwant Bola
- Mr Sohan Marwaha
- Mrs Veerpal Kaur Bhullar
- Mrs Balwinder Ghatohora
- Mr and Mrs Sandhu
- Mrs Rani Neer
- Mrs Ajmer Mahal
- Mrs Gurnam Chandan
- Mr Adrian Walker
- Mr Adrian Wright
- Mr Avtar Singh (Sikh Historian)

For their early review of the manuscript and helpful feedback.

I am indebted to a great author Mrs Rosalind Bradley for providing me with her valuable time and advice and steering me clear of the obstacles she had faced while getting her work published on a similar subject.

It wouldn't have been possible without the support, patience, encouragement, inspiration and dedication of my colleagues, patients, their families and friends, management of LOROS [the hospice], local communities, and of course my own dear family.

There is a special thanks to my dear son Mandeep, being an adviser, graphic designer, proof-reader and above all showering kindness and love with a listening ear whenever I needed it.

How can I forget the advice and guidance of Keith Abbott and Karolina Robinson of Michael Terence Publishing for holding my hand and showing me the tricky path of publishing; being so patient and helpful along the way.

Finally, the warm wishes I have received from the Lord Mayor of Leicester, Baroness Jennifer Gretton a former Lord Lieutenant of Leicestershire, dignitaries, and my loving three grandsons.

Contents

Preface .... *i*
Defining Death *1*
How Do You Define Death? *4*
Three Great Life Lessons from Alexander the Great *10*
Lessons in Loss: What We Can Learn from Grief *13*
The BEST Is Yet to Come! *16*
Volunteering and Donations *19*
Grief, Loss, and Bereavement *47*
The Grief of an Infant Loss *60*
How to Cope with the Grief of Infant Loss *69*
Loss of a Teen *81*
Loss of Parents *88*
Loss of a Spouse/Partner *115*
Loss of a Friend *133*
Suicide *145*
Ways to Cope with Grief and Loss of a Pet *178*
Coping with Cancer *183*
What Happens After Death *197*
I am extremely grateful... .... *230*

Preface

My involvement with the hospice movement was purely accidental. This was the busiest period of my working life. The demand for our services was at its peak and recommendations were coming from all sources. We needed to pick and choose, as I was juggling so many plates at once.

We were renovating the home of a team Captain, who had just won the world cup for England. As usual, I would meet up with him and his wife first thing in the morning and then we would all attend to our commitments for the rest of the day. When I arrived one morning, he was not in his usual cheerful mood and was inattentive to our conversation. When I enquired, he told me that his mother was transferred from hospital to a hospice. He was extremely concerned and needed to visit her that evening. Frankly, I never knew the difference between a hospital and hospice and did not give much thought of its seriousness. We finished our task quickly and I said, "You will be perfectly fine, you shouldn't be worrying, God will look after her."

He replied, "I am not sure, If I could cope, I am a softie at heart and there are going to be so many prying eyes around."

I could see the anguish on his wife's face. I knew the concern was genuine and so I enquired if I can do anything to help.

He turned around and said, "Would you come with me?"

"Definitely," I replied

We set a time to meet each other and I went back to my office. Once I came back to office and told my colleagues about the incident. They all tried to explain to me what a hospice is. All day, I could only think about the hospice, what to expect and what the surrounding and atmosphere would be like. I was now unsure of how I would cope instead of being supporting friend. The day dragged on, I sent someone to buy some flowers, a get-well card and some chocolates.

We met at the carpark. I was nervous and did not know what to say or do apart from just give him a hug. We proceeded to the reception, as we went through the doors the whispers started, even though someone escorted us to the patient's room. People started to gather in the common area and I could see quite a commotion and some were on their phones. Before we knew it, the management arrived and thought I was his (VIP)'s agent. One nurse came forward and said the chief executive would like to have a word with me.

The staff assured us that our privacy would be respected all the time, but if I could talk to this VIP and persuade him to meet with the staff and the management afterwards, 'we are going to arrange some refreshments for you'.

I went back to the patient's room and we spent some valuable time together. I had some discussions with this VIP and without any hesitation he agreed, saying he does this sort of thing regularly and knew how much it matters to these organisations when they receive the encouragement, support and help. He told me to accept the invitation.

I was overwhelmed with the surroundings; it was entirely different to what I had been expecting. There were no screams, no rush or panic. Everyone had a time for the patients, family and friends. The empathy and calm atmosphere was everywhere. But what really struck me was how the place was kept. So many flower arrangements, nicely kept landscaped gardens. There were even pets visiting the patients. Above all, the architectural details were so fine to enhance the surroundings. Every room had a window opens towards the garden and for the relaxation of the patients and visitors there were fish ponds, Avery and quiet areas. There were no restrictions like an ordinary hospital has. As a first impression, I was pleasantly surprised.

After a visit, we were guided to this conference room where

everyone was waiting patiently. The management welcomed us with tea and cakes. They explained how the hospice operates and where the funding was coming from, how the volunteers play a major role in the running of the hospice and what services are provided to the patients, their family and visitors. They also explained what their future goals are.

The VIP got busier with autographs, photos and small conversations; meanwhile I stood in the corner of the room. The Chief Executive walked over to me and said, "I need you to help us."

"I am not a medic; how could I help?" I replied.

But the CEO explained, "I have been watching you all evening: you have managed the situation so well, you are good communicator. Leicester has a large migrant population (approx. 48% migrants living in and around the city) and the irony is even though our services are free, they hardly use the services or participate in any of our activities. I want to change this and I think that you are the person who can."

"But I am shy and not a public person at all; All my life I valued my privacy, to change this, it's going to be difficult". I pointed out my concerns.

"Well, my friend, we do not always know our capabilities. You should consider it and let me know. Spend some time here then make your mind up. I am certain that you will love this challenge." The CEO concluded his conversation as the VIP was eager to leave.

"I will let you know soon." I shock hand with the CEO and joined the VIP to leave the hospice.

That evening; I thought very hard about the hospice movement and the services they provide. Many thoughts ran through my mind, 'what if me or a member of my family needed to use these services; how could I spare time in my busy schedule, all parts of the community need to know about these services, how to access, support and participate in these services'. Regardless of our position, wealth, age, colour, faith and background we all face death and these services are important. Then the biggest factor, which brought it all home to me, was that I myself had recently been faced with a life-threatening health issue, which at the point of diagnosis, was given little chance of survival.

By the morning, my mind was made up and my wife and family encouraged me to accept the position. Well, I do not really know, how I changed, found time and managed to do things, which I thought would have been impossible.

I started to spend three hours every Wednesday, either inviting different communities to the hospice, or I would go to these communities, to talk about the services hospice provides, making notes of their concerns or misconceptions, talking about end of life and death, attending community events as well as visiting different places of worships and arranging fundraising and awareness events.

Before I knew those three hours extended to weekends and other evenings. My family realised that I started to find this work rewarding and encouraged and helped me to become more involved. The work and other commitments were not so important. I found the courage to speak to big or small gatherings and learned how to connect with audiences.

I remember, my first public appearance was at the Leicester City Football Club. The Club declared 'LOROS' as their chosen charity. The chairman and their ambassador lead me out to the centre of the pitch in front of a capacity crowd. After a brief introduction, they told me that I had three minutes to promote our organisation. There was no time to be nervous and I spoke from the heart and when I finished, the crowd applauded and cheered me on a moment that I will never forget.

In the short space of time, the different ethnic communities started to participate, contribute and donate for the organisation; we created a facility which can serve most of the communities in the city. The management listened to the community's concerns and created multifaith services. The communities invited the Hospice to promote their services at places of worships

I benefited personally, learned many new skil s, languages, traditions and customs and even dances. I have built good relations with all the local communities. They respond to our requests whenever we need their help. The minority communities are now an integral part of the organisation.

Defining Death

I have come to realise that the death is indeed a part of my life.

I hear from those who engage with death professionally on a daily basis, those whose lives have been rudely shattered by the sudden loss of a loved one. As I listened to these voices, I found reassurances and enlightenment.

Death is natural, part of our human existence and a great equaliser. Nevertheless, death remains a mystery. What happens when we die? Why do we die? What dies when we die? Is there life after death?

How do we respond to these very human but existential questions? Do we keep them to ourselves? Or do we discuss them with other people and if so, with whom?

Although the answers to these major questions may lie beyond our basic understanding, I have talked to those who are ageing, those suffering from a terminal illness (at any age), those who care for the sick and dying, and those trying to make sense of life and death. They acknowledge the paradox of living and dying. Together with the accompanying feeling of pain, fear, anger and deep sorrow, they recognise that death can also bring a healing, a sense of peace, a meaning to life and sometimes a spiritual awakening or a strengthening of spirit. Death comes to meet us anticipated or not, sometimes it finds us ready and waiting: sometimes it is a surprise and even a shock.

There is importance of preparing for death while continuing to live fully and courageously. Facing death realistically by being grateful for our lives. Letting go of past disappointments, forgiving others and ourselves, and taking care of practical family concerns may help loosen death's stranglehold on us. Recognising death lies beyond our chronology means that at some point we hand over the baton to future generations. This may then help us to become more emotionally and spiritually prepared for death and so lead more fulfilled lives in the present.

In my twilight years, I have found myself thinking about death. strengthen by faith, a long and purposeful life, **I am not frightened of dying.** During my life time, I've had many encounters with death, the anticipated and the unexpected. The question that lingers for us all is how to make sense of death when it comes.

Do not seek death. Death will find you. But seek the road which makes death a fulfilment.

It has encouraged me to live a fuller and more authentic life, and without regrets. I am more sensitive to the need to take care of my relationships, not to leave the love unsaid and to spend some time in daily reflection and meditation. As I grow older it has also led me to ponder what matters most to me and to consider communicating my end-of-life wishes, including advance care planning. I am now more confident about discussing death with family and friends. Coming to terms with death can enrich the meaning of our lives once we become fully conscious that our lifespan is limited and we learn to live more in the present. I believe that death is a natural transition from one stage of consciousness to another.

One scholar wrote it nicely:

"Death is a Comma not a full stop."

How Do You Define Death?

We have not been discussing death, the way we should be. It is like, it never going to happen to us, even if we do acknowledge it, and say yes, we are going to face death, most of us will keep telling ourselves and still believe that it's not **HAPPENING YET.**

It is such a taboo that if someone wants to discuss it, most will try to avoid doing so or try to change the subject, often using humour to deflect the issue *'Why are you being so morbid or stop being so pessimistic'.* Many highly regarded intellectuals' minds have failed to come up with a universal definition of the **DEATH.** There are so many different definitions around, from the medical to spiritual, perceptions are unique to the individual.

Oxford Dictionary

Death noun. the act of dying; the end of life; the total and permanent cessation of all the vital functions of an organism. Compare brain **death**. an instance of this: a **death** in the family; letters published after his **death**.

Medical Definition of Death

Death:

1. The end of life. The cessation of life. (These common definitions of death ultimately depend upon the definition of life, upon which there is no consensus.)

2. The permanent cessation of all vital bodily functions. (This definition depends upon the definition of "vital bodily functions.") See: Vital bodily functions.

3. The common law standard for determining death is the

cessation of all vital functions traditionally demonstrated by "an absence of spontaneous respiratory and cardiac functions."

4. The uniform determination of death. The National Conference of Commissioners on Uniform State Laws in 1980 formulated the Uniform Determination of Death Act. It states that: "An individual who has sustained either (1) irreversible cessation of circulatory and respiratory functions, or (2) irreversible cessation of all functions of the entire brain, including the brain stem is dead. A determination of death must be made in accordance with accepted medical standards." This definition was approved by the American Medical Association in 1980 and by the American Bar Association in 1981.

Death is defined as the act of passing away, the end of life, or the permanent destruction of something.

Should we define death strictly in biological terms? Or the philosophical definition of death? Or on the basis of severe neurological injury even when biological functions remain intact?

Until the mid-twentieth century, the definition of death was frank: a person was pronounced dead when found to be unresponsive and without a pulse or breathing. Two developments encouraged the need for a new concept of death, past the previous definition of death and beyond the philosophical definition of death.

The first development was the invention of mechanical ventilation supported by intensive care, which made it possible to maintain breathing and blood circulation in the body of an individual who would otherwise have died quickly from a brain injury that caused loss of these vital functions. And the second development was organ transplantation, which typically requires the availability of 'living' organs from bodies deemed to be 'dead'.

Philosophical definition of death vs actual death of the brain

Many professors, researchers and scientists have discussed and are still discussing the concept regarding the death of the human brain and are delving further into the **world of neurology. Some reports still uphold the longstanding view that brain death quickly leads to the disintegration of the body, regardless of** medical support, whereas others discuss several cases in which the bodies of patients pronounced brain dead did not 'disintegrate' but were maintained by mechanical ventilation and tube feeding, and others argue that a subset of organ donors – those whose death is declared five minutes after the onset of pulselessness – are not dead because their condition could be reversed with medical intervention.

The concept of being brain dead

The concept of brain death was prominent in conflicts arising after McMath, an America teenager, was declared brain dead in a California hospital in 2013 after complications from elective surgery.

Rejecting this determination, her family moved her to New Jersey, whose brain death statute includes a religious exemption and where a patient covered by this exemption can be enrolled in Medicaid to pay for long-term care.

For nearly four years, McMath was kept biologically alive, until she was declared dead from cardiac arrest in New Jersey in 2018.

The most convincing to my mind is:

"When the Soul departs the body"

The question arises, what is soul? that is another huge subject in itself.

I believe:

The soul is spiritual or immaterial part of all living-beings regarded as immortal.

Death Provides us Wisdom

A ride in Life...

Life is like a journey on a train
With its stations...
With changes of routes...
And with accidents!

We board this train when we are born and
Our parents are the ones who get our ticket

We believe they will always travel on this train with us
However, at some station our parents will get off the train,
Leaving us alone on this journey.

As times goes by, other passengers will board the train
Many will be significant -our sibling, friends, children
And even our love of our life.

Many will get off during the journey and
Leave a permanent vacuum in our lives.

Many will go unnoticed that we won't
Even know when they vacated their seats
And got off the train

This train ride will be full of Joy, sorrow
Fantasy, expectations, hellos
Good-byes and farewells.

A good journey is helping, loving, having a
Good relationship with all the co passengers
And making sure that we give our best to
Make their journey comfortable

The mystery of this fabulous journey is;
We do not know at which station we
Ourselves are going to get off

So, we must live in the best way-adjust
Forget, forgive, and offer the best of
What we have

It is important to do this because when the
Time comes for us to leave our seat...we
Should leave behind beautiful memories for
Those who will continue to travel on the train of life.

Thank you for being one of the passengers on my train.

Have a very pleasant journey of life...

"Death is always a surprise. Not even terminal patients, they think they are going to die in a day or two. In a week, maybe. But only when this particular week is the next week".

We are never ready. It is never the right time. By the time it comes, you will not have done all the things that we wanted to. The end always comes as a surprise.

Three Great Life Lessons from Alexander the Great

Painting by Jean-Simon Berthelemy

I am a big fan of history. I love reading books, listening to legendry tales and documentaries of all kinds of history that has spanned over the centuries. It is fascinating to see how past world leaders, inventors, athletes, armies, scientists, politicians, wars, etc. dealt with the subject of Death.

One of the people who has always fascinated me was Alexander the Great. He was a supreme commander who, believe it or not, was actually tutored under the great philosopher, Aristotle! He wasn't a big man...he was actually a short and stocky man who had two different colour eyes…one brown and one blue. He also founded over 20 cities that bore his name…the greatest being the famous city of Alexandria in Egypt. At the peak of his reign, he ruled over 2007731 square miles of the world!!

So, it is no surprise that when I read the following story about Alexander the Great, it fascinated me and actually reminded me of me some really good concepts and lessons in life, that we all, should never forget.

There is very instructive incident involving the life of Alexander, the great Macedonian king. Alexander, after conquering many kingdoms, was returning home. On the way, he fell ill and it took him to his death bed. With death staring him in his face, Alexander realized how his conquests, his great army, his sharp sword and all his wealth were of no consequence.

He now longed to reach home to see his mother's face and bid her his last adieu. But he had to accept the fact that his sinking health would not permit him to reach his distant homeland. So, the mighty conqueror lay prostrate and pale, helplessly waiting to breathe his last. He called his generals and said, "*I will depart from this world soon, I have three wishes, please carry them out without fail.*" With tears flowing down their cheeks, the generals agreed to abide by their king's last wishes.

"My first desire is that," said Alexander, "My physicians alone must carry my coffin." After a pause, he continued, "Secondly, I desire that when my coffin is being carried to the grave, the path leading to the graveyard be strewn with gold, silver and precious stones which I have collected in my treasury.

"The king felt exhausted after saying this. He took a minute's rest and continued. "My third and last wish is that both my hands be kept dangling out of my coffin. "The people who had gathered there wondered at the king's strange wishes. But no one dare bring the question to their lips.

Alexander's favourite general kissed his hand and pressed them to his heart. "O king, we assure you that your wishes will all be fulfilled. But tell us why do you make such strange wishes?"

At this Alexander took a deep breath and said: "I would like the world to know of the three lessons I have just learnt. I want my physicians to carry my coffin because people should realize that no doctor can really cure anybody. They are powerless and cannot save a person from the clutches of death. So, let not people take life for granted.

The second wish of strewing gold, silver and other riches on the way to the graveyard is to tell People that not even a fraction of gold will come with me. I spent all my life earning riches but cannot take anything with me. Let people realize that it is a sheer waste of time to chase wealth.

And about my third wish of having my hands dangling out of the coffin, I wish people to know that I came empty handed into this world and empty handed I go out of this world."

Alexander's last words: "*Bury my body, do not build any monument, keep my hands outside so that the world knows the person who won the world had nothing in his hands when dying.*"

With these words, the king closed his eyes. Soon he let death conquer him and breathed his last.

Lessons in Loss:
What We Can Learn from Grief

Dealing with grief and loss is a reality we all must confront at some point. The experience of grief is different for everyone, and it has no timetable. Grieving, however, is a necessary part of the coping and healing processes.

The recent death of a friend's son has created within me a vision of the world through which only the lenses of my eyes can see and the beat of my heart can feel. His death has inspired the desire and passion to live my best life every day while giving service to others. This could have easily gone the opposite way, leading to feelings of utter isolation, depression, and loneliness.

For all the pain it brings, grief holds many lessons:

- Grief teaches us that loss is inevitable.
- Grief teaches us not to take loved ones for granted.
- Grief teaches us about our faith.
- Grief teaches us to be patient.
- Grief teaches us that we should live every day creating memories that will comfort us after our loved ones are gone.
- Grief teaches us about our feelings.
- Grief teaches us that it is necessary to grieve. It allows us to move forward.
- Grief teaches us to find our purpose in life.
- Grief teaches us that pain and joy can coexist.
- Grief teaches us to be true to ourselves.

What has your grief taught you?

Verses from Religious Books

We belong to God and to Him we shall return

The Quran 2:156

Yea, though I walk through the valley of shadow of death

I will fear no evil;

For You are with me;

Your rod and staff, they comfort me.

Psalm 23.4

Life, Death and After

May the memory of the life of the departed one be for a blessing
Jewish blessing
Death is nothing but a gateway to birth
Nothing that lives ever dies, it only changes form.
When a man's body is weary the soul leaves
the body to receive newer and fresher garments
And so, on goes this great play of God
From eternity to eternity
Guru Nanak Dev Ji

Never was there a time when I did not exist not you.
Never will there a time hereafter
when any of us shall cease to be.
Bhagavad Gita 2:12

This body is not me
I am not limited by this body
I am life without boundaries
I have never been born
And I have never died
Excerpt from Thich Nhat Hanh

Chanting from the Heart
Buddhist ceremonies and daily practices

The BEST Is Yet to Come!

There was a young man who had been diagnosed with a terminal illness and had been given three months to live. So, as he was getting his things 'in order,' he contacted his Priest and had him come to his house to discuss certain aspects of his final wishes.

He told him which songs he wanted sung at the service, what scriptures he would like read, and what outfit he wanted to be buried in.

Everything was in order and the Priest was preparing to leave when the young man suddenly remembered something very important to him

'There's one more thing,' he said excitedly

'What's that?' came the Priest's reply.

'This is very important,' the young man continued.

'I want to be buried with a fork in my right hand.'

The Priest stood looking at the young man, not knowing quite what to say.

'That surprises you, doesn't it?' the young man asked.

'Well, to be honest, I'm puzzled by the request,' said the Priest.

The young man explained. 'My grandmother once told me this story, and from that time on I have always tried to pass along its message to those I love and those who are in need of encouragement.

In all my years of attending socials and dinners, I always remember that when the dishes of the main course were being cleared, someone would inevitably lean over and say,

'Keep your fork.

'It was my favourite part because I knew that something better was coming… like velvety chocolate cake or deep-dish apple pie.

Something wonderful, and with substance!'

So, I just want people to see me there in that casket with a fork in my hand and I want them to wonder 'What's with the fork?'

Then I want you to tell them:

'Keep your fork… the best is yet to come.'

The Priest's eyes welled up with tears of joy as he hugged the young man good-bye. He knew this would be one of the last times he would see him before his death.

But he also knew that the young man had a better grasp of heaven than he did. He had a better grasp of what heaven would be like than many people twice his age, with twice as much experience and knowledge

He knew that something better was coming.

At the funeral people were walking by the young man's casket and they saw the suit he was wearing and the fork placed in his right hand. Over and over, the Priest heard the question, 'What's with the fork?' And over and over he smiled

During his message, the Priest told the people of the conversation he had with the young man shortly before he died. He also told them about the fork and about what it symbolized to him.

He told the people how he could not stop thinking about the fork and told them that they probably would not be able to stop thinking about it either.

He was right. So, the next time you reach down for your fork let it remind you, ever so gently, that the best is yet to come.

Friends are a very rare jewel, indeed.

They make you smile and encourage you to succeed.

Cherish the time you have, and the memories you share. Being friends with someone is not an opportunity, but a sweet responsibility.

And just remember... keep your fork!

The BEST is yet to come!

Volunteering and Donations

For many years, I worked very closely with Hospice's fund-raising team. Presently, hospices in the UK receive about 30% of their running cost from the UK Government and about 70% comes from fund-raising, donations, legacies and probates etc. I have been fortunate to understand how people get involved in fund raising and donating. Some faiths teach their followers to put aside a percentage of their earning towards charitable causes. Sikhs put aside 10% of their earning. It is well documented that volunteering is good for the body, mind and soul. At our hospice for 31 bedrooms, we have over 1500 volunteers and 342 Paid workers. The volunteers donate, their time, skills, knowledge, products, services and goodwill. It does not matter what the amount or quantity of the donation. I have collected donations of hundreds of thousands from some places and £3 change from infant school children. I remember spending far more time collecting £3 change in pennies than I did collecting a cheque for much larger amount. Talking to young fundraisers seemed far more important to me. Creating and encouraging future fund-raisers, answering their innocent questions, raising awareness about the Hospices outweighed any monetary amount, because you never know where these children will go in their lives. Talking about empathy, life and death and volunteering gave me untold satisfaction. The benefits of volunteering can be enormous. Volunteering offers vital help to people in need, worthwhile causes, and the community, but the benefits can be even greater for you, the volunteer. The right match can help you to find friends, connect with the community, learn new skills, and even advance your career.

Giving to others can also help protect your mental and physical health. It can reduce stress, combat depression, keep you mentally stimulated, and provide a sense of purpose. While it's true that the more you volunteer, the more benefits you'll experience, volunteering doesn't have to involve a long-term commitment or take a huge amount of time out of your busy day. Giving in even simple ways can help those in need and improve your health and happiness.

Benefits of volunteering: 4 ways to feel healthier and happier

1. Volunteering can connect you to others
2. Volunteering is good for your mind and body
3. Volunteering can advance your career
4. Volunteering can bring fun and fulfilment to your life

I wanted to tell you this story, because it is very close to my heart. Few years ago, one of the leading Hollywood Film-makers was interested to make film based on this. She even sent a team to Aberdeen to research the project. Another reason is because the proceeds from main character of the story's estate funded to establish a well-known Hospice in UK.

Some relationships develop by accident, an event or chance meeting that changes people's mindsets and lifestyles beyond their imagination during our lifetime. We never think that it is ever possible, but it does take place. Two individuals met with confrontation at the first meeting and then devoted their entire lives to each other. Our human behaviour towards another human being is like a mirror; it always reflects what we present in front of it. But to bring a change in our attitude requires a challenge, courage, goodwill, and compassion. Sometimes it comes naturally, and other times it comes by someone awakening us. End of life or Death makes us think deeply about our unreasonable behaviour towards any other human- being during our lifetime. We often think we were right, and another person's actions made us behave like that. In reality, we may not have developed a skill to listen to others; we react before we have heard them fully so don't appreciate the other person's point of view. The other person does not have any power to change the person's outlook or person's background, culture, language, or faith. In our minds, we've already built an opinion without any grounds or experience.

This story had taught me many lessons in life. The people who had experienced hardships in their life and needed help and compassion; contributed more generously to the charities. They can value the importance of these institutions clearly better than those who had not used these facilities themselves. I felt that it is important that this story should be included, because it gives a clear message to us that people's attitude, behaviour and mindset can change for better anytime, it only needs an incident.

This is a shortened version of the original...

MASEE (Like Mother)

The train pulled up with a squeak at Guild Street, Aberdeen, Railway Station. It was a lovely August evening. The sun was low and shinning on the granite building creating picturesque reflections. The cool northerly breeze was making it pleasant to walk around the station. A young Sikh stepped down the steps to the platform with a wide smile. He was wearing a printed turban, and smart suit, his eyes were wandering all round as he was looking for someone special. He pulled his suitcase and book bag out of the way of other passengers and taking in the beauty of the building. Suddenly, he felt a tap on his shoulder, a smartly dressed lady with name card in her hand, "are you Ajit?"

"Yes, madam." He replied and extended his right hand to shake her.

She gazed him up from head to toe and surprised to see a young man wearing a turban, a Sikh, she had never seen or talked to a

Sikh before. "I am from university, and I am taking you to your lodging."

"Thank you so much" Ajit, replied, "you have gone through a lot of trouble for me."

"it's a part of the service university provides for our foreign students". She seemed in a hurry and wanted to do her job and attend to her other plans as it was Saturday evening.

"If you gather your belongings and just follow me to my car, we will be on our way".

Ajit was watching everything with an eager eye. The strange people, a peculiar buildings, and unusual outfits. He put the heavy book bag on one shoulder and the suitcase on the other. People were staring at him from all angles. They have never seen a person of colour or a Sikh before in their city. He can hear the whisper among crowds pointing at him. But his enthusiasm was not letting him worry about anything at all; he still remembered the send-off his home town in India had given him.

Ever since he had won a Birla Scholarship, the locals treated him as a legend. [Birla family is one of India's wealthiest industrialists; its company provides 100 scholarships to the top 100 students from all universities in India. The award gave them a chance to study their chosen subject at any university and anywhere in the world. They would pay for all the expenses in return the student needs to serve in one of their companies for five years or pay back two and half times their costs. The town he came from had a population of about seven thousand, but had a college. Nobody in their wildest dreams ever thought that anybody from that town would ever attain a scholarship to a foreign university. Reaching such heights was just not comprehensible to the town folk. When the news came, the people paraded Ajit through the town with pomp and ceremony. The people felt very proud, with almost the everyone congratulated his parents, teachers, and college. It was a great honour and his parents, classmates, and neighbours had never known pride like this. Almost all the town gather to say goodbye at the small local railway station on the day he left. He was loaded with flower garlands around his neck. His classmates were screaming with joy and calling his name; the Priest said prayers, and even the station master decorated his seat.

Ajit wanted to ask her a few questions, but she seemed to be in a hurry. By this time, she was about ten paces in front of him by the time they arrived at her car. Ajit loaded her car's boot and sat at the rear seat. He was looking all around the shining buildings, clean streets and well-kept gardens, quiet roads, and nobody sounding a horn. He asked the lady a few questions about college and studies, and she gave blunt answers as she did not want to enter into long conversation. Soon they reached their destination Cornville Terrace. A row of small terrace houses, two up and two down. Ajit took his belongings out of the car boot, and the lady walked up the path to knock at the door where Ajit was going to stay.

Soon the front door opened; Ajit could hear a commotion coming from the doorway. The landlady had taken a one look at Ajit and started to shout. "I cannot have him here? How come you ever thought that it would be OK to put him here? You have to take this monkey back and put him somewhere else, under no circumstances you can leave him here?"

The lady from the University was trying to calm the landlady down, but she did not want to hear it. Instead, she began to raise her voice more, and the neighbours started to gather to look at what all the commotion was?

Ajit took his bag to the front door and wanted to plead with the landlady before saying anything; she shouted: "take your things back to the car, you are not welcome."

The University lady interrupted, "I cannot stand here for all evening, and I cannot take him anywhere else; you have to take it with the University when it opens on Monday. You may have to pay back the money you collected for his lodging."

"They cannot have it back as I already have spent it" the landlady shouted.

Ajit felt extremely uncomfortable and said, "please explain why you accepted the money if you did not want any lodgers? Now you are saying that you have already spent it; what you expect me to do"?

"I do not care what you do, but you are not staying here that is final," the landlady shouted, as the crowd that had now gathered started to murmur.

Ajit turned around to the University lady and asked, "what do you suggest I should do?"

"Well, it is not up to me, the University's accommodation department has to sort it, my job was to pick you from the station and drop you here. Look, I am already late I have made plans, and my family is waiting for me, I cannot stay here all night" The university lady explained her position.

Ajit realized the situation is grave. He was tired as he had been traveling for over two days straight. He had not eaten for nearly ten hours as well. The lady from the University and the Landlady were not making it easy for him either. He thought that he had to take responsibility to resolve the matter before it accelerates out of hand. He approached the landlady and said, "I realized that you are not happy with me staying here and I accept it, I assure you that come Monday I will go, meanwhile, please let me stay in the room you have already charged us for. I wouldn't bother you at all, I am exhausted, and I will be sleeping in no time, and you wouldn't even know I am here. Let us all accept that we are in this situation not of our making or alternatively you could give me some money to stay in a hotel for a couple of nights".

The landlady, was somewhat surprised at how eloquently Ajit Spoke English, as if she was expecting him to be some sort of jungle savage, she started to realise that she could not afford to put him in a hotel or pay back the money also realized that it was the best way forward and told the lady, so agreed with the lady from the university to go home and she would let him stay until Monday. The Landlady showed Ajit to his room.

Earlier that same day, his father's friend met him at the airport, took one look at him and what he was wearing and led him straight to the Army and Navy Store. Knowing how cold Scotland would be, he bought him a Duffle Coat, four pairs of socks and set of long johns. He also thought of a long train journey ahead, so he treated him to full English Breakfast and a couple of packs of biscuits for the trip.

Ajit did not open his cases after entering the room, he just had the last three biscuits from his handbag and crashed to the bed only momentarily pausing to remove his turban and carefully place it on the desk by the window. He slept like a log, not even the landlady's shouting could have woken him up during the night. However, when he woke up in the morning, the reality of his situation hit him like a ton of bricks

Within two days, he had gone from elation to misery and stark realities of life outside the comfort of his home town had hit him hard. One place on the same earth treating him like a hero and another like an outcast, a lesser being or animal?

He wanted to understand why she behaved that way towards him? But no logical answer was good enough, back home if anyone visited their town regardless of colour, religion or social status, they were treated like guests and Ajit had never faced a similar situation before. The excitement, joy of coming to a so-called civilized country started to evaporate and many questions raced through his head. Why hadn't anybody warned him about this? Would everyone here behave the same way? Why the colour of his skin or turban on his head makes them so uncomfortable? Had he made a wrong decision coming here? What his parents and his classmates think when they would find out the real truth? His world turned upside down. He needed to think hard and quick. He had to find a way forward, reach his goals, and not let down his family, college, friends, and society. He had to face the truth that things would be different, and he had to have a strategy. He had a firm conviction in his faith, and began to pray from his heart and got himself ready. He knew staying any longer in this unwelcoming home would lead to more uneasiness.

He left the house early and wandered around the streets. Being a Sunday morning, it was tranquil and still, deep in his thoughts, he began walking while looking down towards the ground; he heard some singing coming from the nearby Church. He cautiously approached the side door; it was ajar, so Ajit peered in and saw the Priest was delivering a sermon, Ajit felt compelled to enter the hall and found an empty chair near the door. The Priest noticed his presence and acknowledged with eye contact. Once he finished the talk, the Priest announced, "we have a visitor, let us all welcome him to our service" all the congregation turned around and looked at Ajit. The whisper started. The Priest appealed for quiet and requested Ajit to come forward.

"Please tell us your name and where you come from," Priest enquired.

"My name is Ajit Singh, and I am from Punjab, India, I come to study in your beautiful city, in case you are wondering what I am doing here. My parents have told me that I should always pray with the congregation if possible; from my Childhood. I do not know whether anybody else like me is in this city, so I decided to come here; I believed that God listens to your prayers when you pray together. "Ajit said politely and softly.

"What did you pray today?" the Priest inquired.

"It was a private prayer and hoped the God had listened" Ajit replied

"I am sure he had," The Priest assured Ajit.

"I am pleased; I hope that you did not mind me coming like this," Ajit replied.

"Not at all, you are most welcome, and after the service, we will have a talk together, please wait for me the Priest said.

After the service, Priest led Ajit to his residence. He introduced Ajit to his wife and young son. Ajit explained what had happened last night before, and how he was feeling confused and unhappy; he needed some guidance and help. The Priest felt sorry and ashamed to learn about the circumstances and that people from his community had treated him this way. The Priest's wife came and hugged Ajit to comfort him and prepared some sandwiches and a tea as she realized that he had not eaten for so long.

The Priest offered to go with Ajit to reason with the landlady. Landlady hadn't visited the Church for a long time and when she saw a local priest standing on her doorstep with Ajit. She became overwhelmed and flustered, rushing around, she tidied her living room and made room for Ajit and The Priest. The conversation between the Priest and the landlady was very polite and civil. The effect of the Priest's presence and his assurances melted her fears away, removed her anger and she realized that it is best that she honours her commitments and provide a place for Ajit to study. Ajit thanked the Priest and the Landlady. It was then that she introduced herself as Barbara Robinson

That afternoon, Ajit wandered around the garden. He found some necessary tools in the garden shed and some pieces of wood, having grown up on a farm, he soon tidied the shed and sorted the garden even found a time to erect a decent bench to sit on. The neighbours also noticed the changed outlook of the front and rear gardens.

Barbara had a rough upbringing because her parents were not married and gave her up {such was a stigma attached to having a child out of wedlock} was taken into care at birth, and had never met her biological parents. She longed for love and affection during her childhood and youth, but what she got instead, was discipline, punishment, and learning how to evade the authorities. She learned how to survive on the streets and get whatever she needed. Barbara used her good looks to manipulate others and became a ring leader. She has moved from one establishment to the others. She had a reputation for being ruthless and earning a nicknamed "Wild Bab." The punishments or discipline made her strongly opinionated. Barbara had run away from the care homes she grew up in many times. Sooner she reached the age of sixteen; she found a job as a cleaner in the nightclub, where she will hang around to get free drinks or food from the men that frequented it. She was forced to move from one place to another never able to put down roots anywhere. Because of a second world war, the times were hard, and there were not many opportunities around. Aberdeen's shipyard was not big enough to take big ships, and even the granite quarry was not operating fully. The odd ship will come for repairs, and the sailors will come to town and visit the night club where Barbara worked. By now, she has grown into a beautiful young lady, being 5' 10" tall, slim, and knew how to talk to men. She made herself looked more mature than her real age and the sailors were always keen to have her company. Barbara enjoyed her popularity and attention and the men that came to the club would shower her with gifts and money. The other girls in the town were envoy of herself.

One November night in 1944, during a war she met a Navy Officer who fell for her. She also fancied him and started to dream a life with him. He was about 10 yrs. older than her; strong 6'3" bulky American made her weak at the knees. The uniform made her even more smitten and thought it was her opportunity to change her life. Most of the young men around Aberdeen were either serving in the army fighting for king and the country or wasted in the local Quarry with dust and hard labour. Barbara thought God had brought him into her life and was about to change her luck. She was head over heels in love with this American called Simon.

Simon took annual leave while his ship was being repaired and spent every possible moment with her, he took her everywhere, and bought her everything she ever wanted. Then within a few days ship was repaired, and it was time for Simon to sail away. Barbara was gutted, and Simon promised he would keep in touch, and soon the war was over, he would whisk her away to America and settle down. He handed her an emergency telephone number to contact him. They parted with the teary eyes.

She was over the moon with newfound love, but it was soon short-lived she started to feel unwell and realized that she was pregnant. She tried to contact him over and over to deliver the news, but the number never got connected. Barbara's world began to fall apart, again. She was at the same position where her parents were. She was desperate and determined not to let her child go through what she had gone through. The authorities were stringent, and being a Catholic, she was not keen on an abortion. She had done nothing wrong in her mind, and could not let this be public; otherwise, the consequences were not good at all. One evening, she kept thinking she was drowning her sorrows in a local pub and noticed a regular called Tom; who had been coming to this Pub ever since she can remember. He would sit on the same seat for years, just drink his drink and go home without having any conversation with anyone else. He had a steady job at the Granite quarry cutting granite. He had his own house. He always stared at Barbara, what daren't talk. Several times Barbara and her friends made fun of him. She devised a plan, walked to his table, and declared that she was his secret admirer and always wanted to talk to him. He thought all the Christmases came together. If he wanted, he could take her out the coming Saturday, but he had to dress up smart and go away from Aberdeen. Her plan worked, and she convinced him that he had made her pregnant; they need to get married quickly without people knowing just a registrar's office. They got married, and only after seven months a son was born. She named him Simon after the real dad. The people suspected something wasn't right, and Tom also found out the real reason Barbara married him. Barbara and Tom weren't competitive, and their life became one big row. Tom wouldn't accept Simon, his son, and every time they argued, Tom blamed Simon and called him a Bastard. Being both Catholics, they couldn't think to divorce each other; the household became hell on earth. Simon resented being called Bastard, and Barbara would always try to protect him.

When Simon became a teenager, he could not stand it anymore and will get involved regularly. One evening when Tom came from the Pub worse for a drink big argument erupted, and Simon stood up to Tom and scuffle broke out, and there was blood all over the place, Simon got scared that the police will blame him and put him away for a long time in prison. So, he ran away and took a job on a ship and sailed away. That was the last time Barbara seen him. Tom drank himself to the grave soon after. Barbara became a widow at 37. She had the house to herself, and that was when she thought to rent one of her rooms to a student for a regular income and a company.

Well, Ajit knew Barbara had accepted the truce reluctantly, he could not spend too much time at Home, and there were five more weeks before the courses at the University to commence. He had to assess the situation very quickly. In those days a migrant can only bring £3 in cash. Barbara supposed to supply breakfast and evening meal. Ajit knew that the £3 would not last long and he had to find ways to find work and spend the spare time. Even the trees, birds, people all looked strange. There was no telephone service like we have now, and in Ajit's neighbourhood back in India, nobody had a telephone at home. In 1965, you had to write on a particular air letter to a foreign country, and it will take about five to seven days to get there and a similar time to receive a reply. He felt lonely, even though he could write and read English excellently, but he neither could understand the Scottish slang nor speak it. He started to carry a notebook with him so that he can write what he wanted to say. It was too much for 17 years old in a foreign country. The only people he had empathy from, were the local Priest and his wife as they have spent time in India and understood the culture.

Even the priests were very busy in those days Priests and his wife have to perform many duties. Whenever he had time, he would go to the Church and attend to many manual jobs, like gardening, cleaning, decorating, and sorting out the paperwork. Even at home he would ask Barbara if he can do anything for her, slowly she let him decorate the part of the house, and he found some outside paints; there was not a single paint enough to paint the doors of the coal-shed and the outside toilet. So, he painted the doors in a unique pattern that looked amazing and became a neighbourhood talk. A joiner had a workshop nearby and used to walk by Barbara's house and noticed handy decoration. He asked Ajit if he is interested in making Georgian windows, which he accepted thankfully. Now he had work, a place to express his skills. The joiner was very pleased with Ajit's dedication and vision and especially impressed with working out all the figures and designs.

Ajit's room had basic furniture for students' lodging. A second-hand single bed, little desk and chair, and a single wardrobe. He had a small income now. He started to freshen up the room with Barbara's permission, and soon, she liked him to do the other rooms as well. She wouldn't admit, but she was happy with Ajit's presence as there had not been any man around the house for a long while. She started to mellow. They began to have conversations about many topics. She realized that Ajit was finding it quite cold as he came from temperature around 45C, and in Aberdeen, it was only around 10c. She bought him an extra Blanket and got her son's Jumpers. She missed her son and started to find comfort in Ajit's company as she dreamt of Simon's. One day just after the evening meal, she broke down and confessed to Ajit that she is missing Simon, and she is sorry to behave the way she did to him on his arrival. Ajit comforted her, "I am over this now; Mrs. Robinson, please do not worry, no harm had been done; you are like my mum, and no offence been taken."

Barbara inquired, "what you call your mum in your language?"

Ajit felt very emotional; it reminded him of his mum and filled his throat he said: "basically it is not much difference, we call mother 'Ma ji or Bibiji'. 'Masee Ji' is like a mother.

Barbara: "So when you call Mother Ma, and when Bibi and why there always is Ji afterward"?

Ajit: "well 'Ma' when she tells us off and 'Bibi' when we want anything and when she loves us; and 'Ji' for respect. "

Barbara: "that is so nice."

Ajit: "we always speak to our parents with respect, come what may"

Barbara: "You have not told me about MaseeJi."

Ajit: "there is only one Mother, no replacement for her role, but Masee is similar to our Mother, usually a mother's sister. You see, there are two syllables Ma means Mother and See means alike. Being sisters, they are usually alike."

Barbara "I haven't been called Mum for a long time, even when Simon was here; he felt I have not protected him enough and shown the love I should have done" the tears were rolling down her cheeks the hard exterior was melting away in the shape of tears.

Ajit came over and hugged Barbara; "It seemed like centuries since I have spoken to my mum and I am missing her too" both were sobbing and comforting each other.

Ajit: "if you let me, I would like to call you Masee Ji"

Barbara: "that will be so nice, I will love it, really love it, I mean it," and she hugged him tightly. "But No Mrs. Robinson anymore then; I will call you 'Andy' 'cause I can't remember Ajit; usually, aunties give the child a name here."

"Well, that is settled then and let us celebrate with a cup of tea, Andy."

"I will make the tea, and you can find a cake or anything you have, to celebrate, Masee Ji"

Both got up from the settee happily with a new beginning.

Andy started to accept the new surroundings slowly and adopted a routine. Barbara was not ashamed to go by Ajit anymore. They began to shop together and visit other places. She took him to the city centre and shown him where she worked, the famous landmarks. When people asked about Ajit, she would explain proudly that a scholar; who had come to study at our university. Even though she lived in Aberdeen all her life, she never visited Aberdeen University, one day, they went together and explored all the colleges, libraries, gardens, and office buildings. She felt someone special. She took him around the harbour, Union Street, Kings Road, Queens Road, Indoor Market, The famous Lemon Tree Hotel, and the triple Kirk Spire and Church. [Triple kirk Spire has the world's best brickwork]. Going through Queens Street, Barbara mentioned how she and her friends were banned from the street. Only the elite lived in Queen Street, and any riff-raff hanging around here, the police will move them on if you return you got a clip around the ears. She told how many times she had tried and how many times she got caught. Ajit commented why people do this; we all are human, and we need to learn to respect each other regardless of the status or any differences. He also felt confident in exploring the surrounding areas himself.

One evening, he went to the nearby Westburn Park. There were only a few people around. He always felt good in the open spaces; it reminded him of their farm back home. The fresh air and greenery made him relaxed. He will often jog, exercise, explore new plants and trees. It was getting darker and decided to head home. He noticed four young men drinking under a tree and as he was going by them, they all started to run towards him shouting and screaming, he stopped, but they all started to push him around for fun and hit him. He tried to avoid but no avail, he realized that they are not going to stop hurting him. Even though one couple shouted to stop, but their attention was quite clear. The blows and kicks were coming from all directions; he tried to run, but they followed him, and they tried to drag him down to the ground so that they can kick him around like a doll. He noticed a newly planted tree nearby with the tree stake; he ran towards that and grabbed them together. They were trying to pull him away, and during this struggle, the tree-stake came in his hands. He had learned Indian marshal Art Gatka; he used the tree-stake for his defence and fended them away. Because the stake had a sharp end where ever it touched these men, the blood came out, and they got scarred with the site of blood and tried to attend to each other rather than attacking him. Ajit was also covered in blood and looked a mess. He hurried home, and the couple who witnessed everything followed him closely. As he reached home; Barbara heard a loud bang on the door, and soon she opened the door, she was horrified at the site. She screamed, "what happened to you, Andy?" she dragged him inside. His body was black and blue with bruises all over his body; he could hardly speak. She was running around in a panic, thinking of what to do?

Meanwhile, two policemen turned up on the door. "Where is the darky?" one shouted angrily. Barbara thought they come to take his statement or take him to the hospital. They declared that they had come to arrest him as he had bodily harmed four young men with a weapon to her annoyance. She shouted, "have you seen the state of him?

The policeman responded, "I do not know where this animal had come from, but he nearly killed four young men, we will teach him a lesson and teach him how to live in our country. Just hand him over before we forcefully take him". The other policeman pushed his way in and grabbed Ajit by the arm and started to drag him towards their car.

Barbara protested but realized that it was no use, and they were not going to change their mind, and their attentions were not kind. She screamed in anguish and thought the worse, and she grabbed her coat to see what she got to do. The police car disappeared towards the city. She was trembling with emotions. The couple from the park arrived and told in detail what had happened. Now she was extremely fearful; she ran to the nightclub where she worked as a cleaner. Good three miles away. Out of breath, she knocked on the door of the owner of the club.

"Ralph, Ralph, please help me, help me. I beg you," she could hardly stand straight.

"Barbara, calm down, tell me what had happened, you are not making any sense?" Ralph enquired.

"I do not know what they are going to do to my Andy"? Barbara pleaded.

"Who Is Andy" Ralph wanted to know more. Please take a glass of water and explain it to me properly. Barbara explained everything and begged Ralph to provide bail for Andy.

Ralph went to the police station with Barbara and got Ajit bailed out with £50 bail and dropped both of them back at her Home.

"Barbara, do not worry; just look after him, and I will talk to my solicitors tomorrow, he realized how bad Ajit looked, I do not think anything will come of it, soon they realized what had happened" Ralph assured both. "I will come around in the morning to check how he is?"

Barbara and Ajit thanked Ralph.

It was a difficult night for both of them. Ajit developed a

temperature, and Barbara spent all night nursing his injuries. She could not figure out whether something was broken or damaged. There was swelling and bruising to both Ait's eyes; cut and swollen nose, being sick repeatedly and cringng with pain when she touched him. She was frightened with fear. She was not sure what she should be doing? Probably, the first time in her life, she prayed. Her thoughts were with Ajit's family. She wanted to do her best to make sure that she had done everything possible.

She heard a milkman at her door she ran to catch him before he left to inform the Priest for advice and help. At the daybreak the Priest arrived, he was horrified by the look of Ajit's condition. He realized that Ajit needed urgent help and comfort. He ran back home and called the ambulance and register Ajit with his GP. Barbara went with Ajit to the hospital. They checked him over, luckily found nothing broken what his body was bruised internally and externally. They kept him in hospital for observation for the next three days. All the neighbours had heard what had happened by now. They all were feeling sorry and concerned about Ajit's well- being. On his return home, most of them brought him food, handwritten get well cards and flowers.

The police had enough witnesses who came forward to verify what had happened. The local bobby came around and informed that there would be no case for Ajit to answer. The Priest and Barbara were anxious about Ajit's safety now. The local press came to interview him so that the readers in the city come to know who Ajit was and what had happened to him. It became front-page news. Many readers offered stories relating to their Sikhs' experiences either during the wars or during the British Raj. Most of them commented on his innocence as it was printed in his story how he selected Aberdeen instead of other word famous Universities.

"he and his principal made a choice based on the British universities list supplied by the British Embassy in Delhi India.

The list was prepared alphabetically, and at number one was Aberdeen University; they all thought that Ajit was going to Number one university in the UK."

After this unfortunate episode, Barbara would not let him own his own, and she tried to shadow him everywhere. Ajit and Barbara went to see Ralph to thank him for his generosity and kindness. Ajit offered to help him in any way he could. Ralph was struggling with his accounts; his bookkeeper being on holiday, and Ajit stepped in. To Ralph's surprise, Ajit sorted all his filing, accounts and tidied his office the way he had not seen before. Ajit made all the spreadsheets to show him all aspects of his business's finance the way he has never seen. He was extremely impressed with his math knowledge and approach. He offered him a regular job to help his existing staff. Ajit had to choose between a joiner's help or office help, but it was a natural choice to show his gratitude for Ralph's offers, but he was reluctant to accept payment for it.

The term at the University started, and Ajit had to face all kinds of questions and adjustments. In 1965, only people from the well to do families went to universities. Only a few can afford to go. All his classmates had a story to tell who they were and what their families did. He had to make his place among the other students. It did not take long as his teachers spotted his exceptional mathematical talent and unique way of solving complicated problems. One of the teachers was so impressed that she wanted to demonstrate to others. There were no calculators around, and he can solve the sums, multiplication, divisions, and subtractions in a blink of an eye. One day in a morning assembly, she presented Ajit and invited questions from students and teachers. He answered everything correctly at a fantastic speed. She declared afterward that the methods he used she never came across. After this, Ajit did not need any introduction; other students offered friendship in return of help with their work. Some of them had read his story in the newspaper and wanted to show that not all the peoples are same, good and bad are in every community. The college offered him free course books, and teachers offered him help. He had a lot to learn about British culture and others about him. He was missing his favourite Cricket, and not many people in Aberdeen had an Interest in Cricket, but it was not long before there was a cricket team in a university.

Ajit adjusted to his new normal quickly, and it was pleasant for him. He had a regular income from his job as an office helper. Ralph started to pay him generously as his prepared projection sheet made it very easy for him to convince the banks or Building Societies to lend him for his future investments. His accountants were pity impressed too. He recognized his talent, which was helping him to progress at a faster rate than ever before. Ajit's studies were going fine; the teachers were delighted. He did not need to ask for more money from back Home for his education and living. He had a group of friends and teachers who would help him whenever he needed it.

During this period, he started to find out where other migrants lived and where he could get the spices to make food he was used to. He was missing his culture, language, traditions, festivals, music, and people. He found out there were Punjabi newspaper and weekly magazines in England; so, he wrote to his father's friend to send him some. He started to write for these papers and magazines about his experiences in Aberdeen. He had followers, and he found the sources where he can get the things he was missing. He arranged a regular parcel service from England to have Asian foods and spices. He introduced these spices at home first, Barbara loved it and wanted more and more. Her favourite soups, casseroles, and other dishes started to taste differently. Barbara was so excited about new adventures she began to announce to her neighbours. The demand grew. Ajit came with the idea to introduce the spicy Soup to the university canteen it went better than they expected. Then a new venture started. Barbara would prepare the Soup, and Ajit will add spices and pot of Soup would end up in the canteen every morning. Within the first hour, it would get sold out. The demand exceeded supply. Barbara started to get a good return, and soon, she hired help, and two pots were delivered daily and she left the cleaning job that she did not enjoy much as she had to clean after the punters being sick, urinated or blood from their fights at the night club. The more significant cooking facilities were created, and Ajit negotiated a good deal with the indoor market's café in the city centre to supply a special soup named Masee. Barbara bought a little van and got busy providing the Soup, and Masee soup was born.

Ajit's studies finished; he even managed an extra course; now, he was a qualified Architect and Quantity Surveyor. He had the top marks, and all his classmates and teachers were very proud of him. He came as a stranger to Aberdeen but became one of the famous citizens. None happier for him than Barbara, the Priest, and Ralph. He came as a naïve, innocent young man, but became a sophisticated graduate ready to face the world. He had the big decision to make whether to return to India and work for his sponsors or stay in the UK. Barbara did not want him to go; she found stability in her life; she only dreamt. He was missing his family; they wanted him to come back but realized that he had more chances in the UK than in India. Barbara and Ajit had a heart-to-heart discussion about the prospects on either side of the pond. She and Ralph offered to pay back his sponsors to stay here. Ralph even offered him a job in his business. Ajit found all the options open to him and decided that he would stay in the UK but move to England as there were more opportunities.

Before he left Aberdeen, he made a deal for Barbara's business to have a steady income. The café where she was supplying Soup, the lease was up for renewal soon, and the present occupier wanted to retire. So Ajit prepared all the paperwork for Barbara to have a long favourable lease on her name and sorted out the business model. The local people supplied Homemade food and more seating for the customers were created. Barbara, now was a proper business lady, respected Mrs. Robinson.

Ajit selected to come to Leicester as he had his fellow villagers settled there. The living cost was cheaper than London and it was convenient to commute either to the South or North. Almost all his classmates were handpicked by the international companies but Ajit could not land a job. On a paper, he was every firm's choice and sooner he turned up for interviews; all sorts of excuses came up. But he was determined not to accept failure; he knew the culture, system and had qualifications to offer. Barbara was very supportive. She kept in touch by ringing him every day and offering a word of advice. Ajit took all sorts of manual jobs but kept applying for a job in his field. He stood on the market stall, drove Buses, decorated houses, delivered leaflets. In those days for educated migrants, it was considered a good job if you worked on the buses or the post office. He would drive buses at night and do the job hunting during the day.

The migrant communities were beginning to settle down in the UK, making their Home; rather than migrant labour. They were trying to create community centres and religious places for their respective communities. Ajit offered them his services as an Architect on a volunteer basis to stay in touch with recent regulations. All the city communities respected his services, which came very handy when he established himself later in life. Nearly two years passed in this struggle, and one day out of a blue, a letter arrived; from the firm he applied previously wanted him to come for a discussion. In Midland, the government wanted to build a new hospital and invited designs from all the known firms. This firm had not designed any hospital before and did not want to miss this business opportunity. So, they told Ajit to create a design and submit if his design got selected, then they will offer him a position. The firm will supply all the support required. Ajit took this challenge and started to work on the design; he asked help from his classmates who were working for established firms worldwide. He created a straightforward design and uniquely convenient for the workers. The build cost was 40% less than the nearest competitive. The firms from all over the globe tendered for this work, but the committee selected Ajit's design.

Now Ajit was in an excellent position to ask for his employment terms. Ralph and Barbara were supporting him all the way. He demanded to be an equal partner with the two-existing partner of this one of Leicester's most prominent Architectural firm, or he will go on his own to compete with them. The existing partners were not happy about this and but did not want to lose this opportunity. Hence, they came up with an unrealistic counteroffer and asked £75000.00 for 1/3 share of the company, and it needed to be paid within four weeks; otherwise, he can work as an employee on their term. At that time, you could buy an excellent detached house with a garage for £3500.00. They knew he could not raise money like this in the specified time. Ajit tried all the banks; no bank wanted to lend that sort of money without any security. He was desperate now, and did not know what to do? One day, he picked up the courage to discuss with Barbara; she offered to sell her house and business; what it wouldn't be enough, she suggested Ajit to talk to Ralph. Ralph knew Ajit would not do anything if it were not feasible, so he arranged a ten-year loan. Ajit surprised the firm and became a third partner in the firm.

His designed hospital is still regarded as one of the outstanding designs for a hospital, and the floodgate opened for the firm to create more hospitals and other medical facilities. The firm became known globally for medical establishments. The firm had won nine awards for its designs to date. Barbara acquired the neighbouring building to extend her café and bought a house in Queens Road with the help of Ajit. Because of the listed street, he could not alter the exterior, but he created design and landscapes, which became the city's talking point. The girl [Wild Bab] banned from the street in her earlier life was the proud owner of this property. Ajit returned the loan to Ralph in just four years. Ajit went back home to marry his childhood sweetheart, and when returned, Barbara invited the couple to her Home and thrown a party to remember. Most of the VIPs from Aberdeen turned up; Barbara was well connected in the city now.

Barbara and Ajit felt a part of a family. They shared their happiness and sorrows. Barbara's son never contacted her. She often wondered about him. She became God- Mother to Ajit's two sons, and Ajit's family always loved and respected Barbara as a family member. Ralph became one of the wealthiest person around Aberdeen. He still regarded Ajit as his inspiration. The Priest and his family also kept in touch with Ajit's family. The memories of Aberdeen were always sweet to everyone.

Even though Ajit had a good exercise routine, but the stress from busy work and growing family caused him to suffer a massive stroke in 1996, He lost a speech, and one side was paralyzed, the recovery was slow. He could not travel or speak on the phone while Barbara was diagnosed with cervical cancer. They wanted to comfort each other but unable to do so, due to their circumstances. It was a strange and sad situation. Barbara's carer and Ajit's family knew the heartache they both been suffering. Ajit's condition improved after ten months, and he decided to visit Barbara as her health was deteriorating rapidly and admitted to care home instead of her own house. She wanted Ajit to sort out so much, and she knew there was not much time.

Ajit and Barbara had a tearful reunion, and they held to each other for a long time, reliving all the ups and downs of their respective lives. The care home manageress handed Ajit a big bundle of letters. He started to pile those up in different piles and came across one from an Australian TV's company producer. They had a live program on their channel locating lost relations. An Australian Actress won the Oscar for a supporting role in Hollywood movies; according to their research, the actress is a granddaughter of Barbara. They wanted her to appear on their show and reunite granddaughter and Grand mum first time in their lives. He put that letter aside. After dealing with everything else and having instructions from Barbara on every issue, he decided to discuss this important letter. He was mindful that her health was delicate, and it had to be done sensitively.

"Hi, Masee, I have a crucial thing to discuss with you" Ajit's voice was strutting due to stroke

"Andy, do not tell me that I am dying. I know that" after a little pause, "I am prepared now," Barbara replied.

"No, Masee, it is not such the bad news, that someone found your granddaughter, Simon's daughter," Ajit Squeezed her hand softly.

Barbara quickly sat down with excitement, "tell me that you are not joking Andy."

Ajit: "Would I joke about something like this"

Barbara: "Where?"

Ajit: "I do not know exactly, somewhere in Australia."

Barbara; "Damn, why it has to be that far? Don' t you remember Andy, I always said that one day I would find him."

Ajit: "Mother always has the instinct."

Barbara; "What you think we should do, Andy?"

Ajit: "You tell me Masee"

Barbara: "Let us go, but you have to come with me."

Ajit: "let me make all the arrangements, and you get your best dress ready, and we are going to be a TV stars, soon".

After a few days, they travelled to Sydney. The journey was tiring and long. The production team came to meet them at the hotel and briefed them on what would happen. Barbara was anxious and tired. She wanted to prepare what to say. She has gone to sleep early, and the producer told Ajit; what they found in their research.

According to the producer, Simon ended up near Brisbane on a farm. He worked as a farmhand. He married the farmer's daughter. He was notorious for his hard-drinking, working, and fighting. They had a daughter called Amy. But their married life was troublesome; he was often thrown out of a farm by his wife's family. Amy was about four when he got into a fight with two brothers in a bar, and they stabbed and killed him. Amy 's Mother married again, and Amy had two stepbrothers. Her Mother hadn't talked much about Simon. I suppose bad memories. But she always told Amy that her dad used to say that his Mother was one of the best-looking women in Aberdeen and Amy looked just like her.

Next evening the makeup teamed worked their wonders on Barbara. Barbara wore a royal blue long dress and 3" high heels. The pure white pearls and white sparkling small purse. Due to her illness, she lost weight and looked nothing less than a model on the cat-walk. Ajit had a red turban and cream-coloured, beautifully tailored suit. Ajit had Barbara on his arm, and both turned the audience's heads around with their classy gate. They were greeted with loud applause. Amy was called to the show on a pretence that she had to introduce a Scottish lady to her granddaughter. When Amy appeared on the stage, you can tell they were a carbon copy of each other. Both could not take eyes from each other. When the truth emerged, there wasn't a dry eye in the audience. They clung to each other like a sweet peas' clings to a frame. Nobody was acting, and it was really raw emotions on display. Ajit noticed it was too much for Barbara and suggested that we go to the hotel and catch up with the lost time there.

Amy climbed up to Barbara's bed, and they were speaking for a while then kissing each other and another question will come up. Even though Amy had not had her dad around her, when growing up, you can tell she missed that. Barbara kept repeating, "I loved Simon so much. I wish I could have told him earlier". Ajit was watching this touching moment and noticed all of a sudden

Barbara gone quiet. When he touched her body, it was cold. "Amy, Amy, Barbara had left us, but she was so happy" Ajit pulled Amy away.

Amy found out about Ajit and Barbara's relationship and she was so thankful that she had met her Grand mum and thanked Ajit to made it possible. Amy asked Ajit if she could have her grandma buried near her Home in Sydney to visit her. Ajit stayed for the funeral. They found two letters from her purse, which she was carrying for a while one was for Simon and one for ANDY [Ajit]. Because she was hoping that Simon maybe somewhere in Australia and it just said: "I love you and I always did".

The other one for Ajit said, "Andy, please forgive me, how I had treated you on the first instance. I did not know that you were my Angel and would fulfil my dreams, here is a letter of Authority to do whatever you like with whatever I have, actually you have created it. One more thing you gave happiness I never experienced before. I hope I had been a good Masee. Well, I will wait till we meet again."

Ajit sold her estate and, with the proceeds, built a Hospice in her name in Scotland.

Grief, Loss, and Bereavement

Most people will experience **loss** at some point in their lives. **Grief** is a reaction to any form of loss. **Bereavement** is a type of grief involving the death of a loved one.

Bereavement and grief encompass a range of feelings from deep sadness to anger. The process of adapting to a significant loss can vary dramatically from one person to another. It often depends on a person's background, beliefs, and relationship to what was lost.

GRIEVING THOUGHTS AND BEHAVIOURS

Grief is not limited to feelings of sadness. It can also involve guilt, yearning, anger, and regret. Emotions are often surprising in their strength or mildness. They can also be confusing. One person may find themselves grieving a painful relationship. Another may mourn a loved one who died from cancer and yet feel relief that the person is no longer suffering.

People in grief can bounce between different thoughts as they make sense of their loss. Thoughts can range from soothing ("She had a good life.") to troubling ("It wasn't her time."). People may assign themselves varying levels of responsibility, from "There was nothing I could have done," to "It's all my fault."

Grieving behaviors also have a wide range. Some people find comfort in sharing their feelings among company. Other people may prefer to be alone with their feelings, engaging in silent activities like exercising or writing.

The different feelings, thoughts, and behaviors people express during grief can be categorized into two main styles: instrumental and intuitive. Most people display a blend of these two styles of grieving:

- **Instrumental grieving** has a focus primarily on problem-solving tasks. This style involves controlling or minimizing emotional expression.
- **Intuitive grieving** is based on a heightened emotional experience. This style involves sharing feelings, exploring the lost relationship, and considering mortality.

No one way of grieving is better than any other. Some people are more emotional and dive into their feelings. Others are stoic and may seek distraction from dwelling on an unchangeable fact of living. Every individual has unique needs when coping with loss.

MODELS OF GRIEF

Grief can vary between individuals. However, there are still global trends in how people cope with loss. Psychologists and researchers have outlined various models of grief. Some of the most familiar models include the five stages of grief, the four tasks of mourning, and the dual process model.

THE KÜBLER-ROSS MODEL OF GRIEF

Loss can leave us with a wide range of emotions. The experience of each emotion signals that a deep bond has been broken. One day we may be in denial, anger, or depression. Other days, we might feel like we can go on. Until, that is, the cycle starts all over again.

In her 1969 book On Death and Dying, psychiatrist Elisabeth Kübler-Ross introduced what came to be known as the "five stages of grief," which represent the typical series of experiences for those who have faced loss:

1. **Denial:** "This isn't happening."
2. **Anger:** "How could this happen?"
3. **Bargaining:** "Please make this not happen. In return I will ___."
4. **Depression:** "I'm too sad to do anything."
5. **Acceptance:** "I'm finally at peace with what happened."

As stated earlier, each person experiences grief in different ways. Thus, it's important to emphasize that while the Kübler-Ross model serves as a general guide for how grief is often processed, not everyone experiencing grief or loss may experience every stage, let alone in order.

HOW TO HELP A GRIEVING FRIEND

If someone you know has lost a loved one, the following

suggestions may help:

- **Listen:** Follow the advice of musician Michael McLean. When someone is grieving, "show up and shut up." The grief-stricken person needs to be heard and feel that someone cares. Grief is a personal experience, an experience that belongs solely to the person experiencing it, and you must allow them the respect and time they deserve. Listening to someone who grieves is an invaluable gift.

- **Be a gatekeeper:** In an intensely painful and overwhelming time, offer to be the person through which information is filtered for dissemination. You may find that other friends, family members, and acquaintances ask for information about your friend. Normalize grief with responses such as, "They have good days and bad days—and probably will for a long time." Or, "Grief never really ceases. It is something you carry with you in different ways for the rest of your life."

GETTING SUPPORT FOR GRIEF

The grieving process can be long and lonely. If you are grieving, take the time you need, meet any challenging emotions that arise within you with self-compassion, and accept support from others. Talking about grief is an important part of healing. Receiving reassurance and feeling empathy expressed for your loss may help make the recovery process seem a little less daunting. If you need or desire further support, I strongly encourage you to contact a licensed therapist who works with grief and loss.

Four Tasks of Mourning

Psychologist J. W. Worden also created a stage-based model

for coping with the death of a loved one. He divided the bereavement process into four tasks:

- To accept the reality of the loss
- To work through the pain of grief
- To adjust to life without the deceased
- To maintain a connection to the deceased while moving on with life

Dual Process Model

As an alternative to the linear stage-based model, Margaret Stroebe and Hank Schut developed a dual process model of bereavement. They identified two processes associated with bereavement:

Loss-oriented activities and stressors are those directly related to the death. These include:

- Crying
- Yearning
- Experiencing sadness, denial, or anger
- Dwelling on the circumstances of the death
- Avoiding restoration activities

Restoration-oriented activities and stressors are associated with secondary losses. They may involve lifestyle, routine, and relationships. Restoration-oriented processes include:

- Adapting to a new role
- Managing changes in routine
- Developing new ways of connecting with family and friends
- Cultivating a new way of life.

Stroebe and Schut suggest most people will move back and

forth between loss-oriented and restoration-oriented activities.

THE PROCESS OF RECOVERING FROM GRIEF

Everyone grieves in their own way and in their own time. Some people recover from grief and resume normal activities within six months, though they continue to feel moments of sadness. Others may feel better after about a year.

Sometimes people grieve for years without seeming to find even temporary relief. Grief can be complicated by other conditions, most notably depression. The person's level of dependency on the departed can also cause complications.

The grieving process often involves many difficult and complicated emotions. Yet joy, contentment, and humour do not have to be absent during this difficult time. Self-care, recreation, and social support can be vital to the recovery. Feeling occasional happiness does not mean a person is done mourning.

Grieving the loss of a loved one be a difficult process, whether the loss is due to death, a breakup, or other circumstance. One of the hardest challenges is adjusting to the new reality of living in the absence of the loved one. Adjusting may require a person to develop a new daily routine or to rethink their plans for the future. While creating a new life, a person may adopt a new sense of identity.

COMPLICATED GRIEF

The experience of grief is not something a person ever recovers from completely. However, time typically tempers its intensity. Yet an estimated 15% of people who have lost a loved one will experience "complicated grief." This term refers to a persistent form of bereavement, lasting for one year or more.

Again, the length of time it takes for a person to grieve is highly variable and dependent on context. But when symptoms persist without improvement for an extended period, they may qualify as complicated grief. In addition, the symptoms of complicated grief to be more severe. Complicated grief often dominates a person's life, interfering with their daily functioning.

Prolonged symptoms may include:

- Intense sadness and emotional pain
- Feelings of emptiness and hopelessness
- Yearning to be reunited with the deceased
- Preoccupation with the deceased or with the circumstances of the death
- Difficulty engaging in happy memories of the lost person
- Avoidance of reminders of the deceased
- A reduced sense of identity
- Detachment and isolation from surviving friends and family
- Lack of desire to pursue personal interests or plans

The Diagnostic and Statistical Manual (DSM-5) does not classify complicated grief as a clinical condition. Yet it does include diagnostic criteria for "persistent complex bereavement disorder" in the section of conditions requiring further study.

BROKEN HEART SYNDROME

Generally speaking, grief cannot kill a person. That said, there are cases in which severe stress could harm an otherwise healthy person's heart.

When a person experiences a shocking event, their body fills with stress hormones. These hormones can cause part of a person's heart to briefly swell and stop pumping. The rest of the heart continues beating, causing blood to flow unevenly. A person may feel intense chest pain, similar to a heart attack (but unlike a heart attack, the arteries are not blocked). This temporary malfunction is called "broken heart syndrome."

As the name suggests, the broken heart syndrome often follows news of loss, such as a <u>divorce</u> or death of a loved one. Yet symptoms can also appear after a good shock, such as winning the lottery. Women are more likely than men to develop the condition.

Most people who experience broken heart syndrome recover within weeks. Deaths from the condition are rare. Since the syndrome is prompted by a shocking event, people have a low risk of experiencing it twice.

DEPRESSION AND GRIEF

The DSM-5 does not define bereavement as a disorder. Yet typical signs of grief, such as social withdrawal, can mimic those of <u>depression</u>.

So how can one tell the difference between grief and depression?

- Grief is typically preceded by loss. Depression can develop at any time.
- The sadness present in grief is typically related to the loss or death. Depression is characterized by a general sense of worthlessness, despair, and lack of joy.
- Symptoms of grief may improve on their own with time. Someone with depression often needs treatment to recover.

Despite their differences, depression and grief are not

mutually exclusive. If someone is vulnerable to depression, grief has the potential to trigger a depressive episode. If someone already has depression, their condition may prolong or worsen the grieving process. A therapist can help a person in mourning recognize and manage any depressive symptoms.

BEREAVEMENT AND CULTURE

Certain aspects of grief are virtually universal. Most cultures have rituals of mourning after a death. Crying is common, regardless of a person's origins. However, the bereavement process can vary dramatically depending on one's culture. Cultural values may affect a person's:

- **Attitude toward death**: Many Western cultures display death-denying traits. Death is often depicted as something to fight or resist. Eastern cultures, meanwhile, tend to characterize death to be a part of life. Death is often considered more of a transition than an end. Research suggests people in death-denying cultures tend to have more anxiety around death than people in death-accepting cultures.

- **Remembrance of the deceased**: Some cultures, such as the Hopi or Achuar peoples, grieve by attempting to forget as much of the deceased as possible. It may be taboo for loved ones to say the person's name or to touch their belongings. Rituals are done to sever connections with the dead. Other cultures mourn by sharing memories of the deceased. People in the Akan region of Ghana often hold elaborate funerals which may cost a full year's income. The deceased are typically placed in "fantasy coffins" personalized with symbols of their life.

- **Emotional Displays**: Social norms can differ regarding how much emotion is "appropriate" to show. A 1990 study compared bereavement norms in two Muslim societies. Mourners in Egypt may be encouraged to grieve for an extended period of time. A person might display their love for the deceased through displays of unrestrained emotion. Meanwhile, Balinese culture tends to pathologize overt sorrow. People are encouraged to put on a happy face in front of others and to cut ties with the deceased.

When analysing grieving behaviors, context matters as much as the symptoms themselves. Bereavement trends which are typical in one culture may be stigmatized in another. When working with individuals in grief, therapists may need to keep cultural influences in mind.

DISENFRANCHISED GRIEF

Disenfranchised grief occurs when a person's mourning is restricted in some way. Society may stigmatize a person's mourning process or refuse to acknowledge their loss. Grief may be disenfranchised for several reasons:

- **Society devalues the loss**. The loss of a pet often garners less sympathy than the loss of a human relative. Others may say "it was just an animal" and accuse the person of being too emotional. Yet research shows the mourning period for a pet is about the same length as for a human family member.

- **The loss is ambiguous**. An adopted child may grieve the loss of their birth parents, even if said adults are alive. If a loved one has late-stage dementia, family members may feel as if the person they knew is gone.

- **Society stigmatizes the circumstances of the loss**. Pregnancy-related loss is often considered taboo. Women who undergo a miscarriage may feel guilt and shame. They may avoid telling others about the loss to avoid being blamed.

- **Society doesn't recognize the person's relationship to the deceased**. A co-worker or friend may mourn a person, but they will likely receive less support than a family member. The same is true for ex-spouses, even though they used to be family. In societies with systemic homophobia, same-sex partners may also have disenfranchised grief.

- **Others do not consider the person capable of grief**. When young children experience loss, adults may misinterpret signs of bereavement. They may believe the child is not capable of understanding the loss or have prolonged feelings about it. People who have cognitive impairments or intellectual disabilities may also have disenfranchised grief.

Disenfranchised grief can interfere with the bereavement process. If society does not recognize a loss, the person may have trouble accepting it themselves. They may try to repress or deny their emotions. Shame and secrecy can make the symptoms of grief more severe.

Social support is often vital to recovery. A community can provide emotional and financial aid when people are vulnerable. Mourning rituals can offer closure. If a person is forced to grieve alone, they may have a delayed recovery.

If you have lost someone or something precious, you may wish to find a therapist. Therapy can help with any sort of loss, whether society validates the grief or not. Therapy is an opportunity to explore your feelings and memories without judgment. No loss is too big or too small to warrant support. You do not have to endure your grief alone.

References:

1. Doka, K. (2002). Disenfranchised Grief. In K. J. Doka (Ed.), *Living with Grief: Loss in Later Life* (pp. 159-168). Washington, D.C.: The Hospice Foundation of America.

2. Gilbert, K. (2007, August 26). *HPER F460/F450: Ambiguous Loss and Disenfranchised Grief, unit 9 notes*. Retrieved from http://www.indiana.edu/~famlygrf/units/ambiguous.html

3. Gire, J. (2014). How Death Imitates Life: Cultural Influences on Conceptions of Death and Dying. *Online Readings in Psychology and Culture, 6*(2). Retrieved from https://scholarworks.gvsu.edu/cgi/viewcontent.cgi?referer=https://www.google.com/&httpsredir=1&article=1120&context=orpc

4. Is broken heart syndrome real? (2017, December 12). American Heart Association. Retrieved from http://www.heart.org/HEARTORG/Conditions/More/Cardiomyopathy/Is-Broken-Heart-Syndrome-Real_UCM_448547_Article.jsp#.Ww3GkUgvyM8

5. Kersting, K. (2004, November). A New Approach to Complicated Grief. *Monitor on Psychology, 35*(10). Retrieved from https://www.apa.org/monitor/nov04/grief.aspx

6. Klass, D., Silverman, P. R., & Nickman, S. L. (1996). *Continuing bonds: New understandings of grief.* Philadelphia, PA: Taylor & Francis

7. Major Depressive Disorder and the "Bereavement Exclusion". (n.d.) American Psychiatric Association. Retrieved from http://www.dsm5.org/Documents/Bereavement%20Exclusion%20Fact%20Sheet.pdf

8. Wakefield, J. C. (2013). DSM-5 grief scorecard: Assessment and outcomes of proposals to pathologize grief. *World Psychiatry*. Retrieved from http://www.ncbi.nlm.nih.gov/pmc/articles/PMC3683270

9. Why we need to take pet loss seriously. (2018, May 22). *Scientific American*. Retrieved from Dishttps://www.scientificamerican.com/article/why-we-need-to-take-pet-loss-seriously

The Grief of an Infant Loss

I always have been intrigued to find out how the professionals are dealing with death on daily basis. How they feel, cope or understand this universal fact. Detachment is not always easy. Afterall we are all humans and the professionals also have their family, friends, relations, their favourite social and religious leaders, artists, teachers and role models.

How they deliver the news of death? How they console and sympathise with the relatives and friends? What language they use? What is their mechanism to dealing with when they get effected with the trauma or overwhelmed with the occasion?

As a psychotherapist, I often talk to the bereaved about their memories of their loss. Surprisingly, we never forget the time, date, weather, location or when we receive the news of a death.

Most of the people will always remember what was said and who said it. It is such an event that we also remember how we reacted. Most of the bereaved remember how their loved one was treated by the professionals and hospitals. Professionals' empathy, professionalism or their neglect mis-behaviour, treatment, care and the place where the death occurred, plays a big role in our grief.

There are occasions when we just behave like humans not as a professional. Our feeling takes over and we try to cover our emotions. The professionals are not actors and they also have feelings. They also get effected in a big way and they require treatment themselves. There are so many facilities available to help them but often their resilience or experience make them hesitant to access the help.

I want to share with you what I been told.

Deborah de Wilde OAM

Former midwife and social worker

"Birth and death are usually two distinct events separated by many years of a life hopefully well lived. When the birth and death collide, the pain. Shock and confusion are devastating.

How can parents make sense of this?

My contact with a family may begin soon after the ultrasound and confirms an unborn baby's death. At other times I may be summoned to support a family who is being transferred to a theatre for the urgent delivery of their baby, or to be with a family whose new born is gravely ill. To say that I meet parents at a time of enormous stress is a massive understatement.

They might be sitting alone in a delivery suite, dry- eyed, silent, stunned having just been told that their yet-to-be-born or newly born baby has died. At other times the parents' anguish is immediate and I may enter the room to the cries of the mother howling, pleading for a reprieve from the knowledge of her baby's death, begging for the truth to be reversed.

Devastating news followed by interventions and decisions. All around them the business of the hospital and world continues unabated.

When I am with a family, I explain I will be there for them and that there will be much for us to discuss, that we will go slowly and gently and at their pace. A sense of trust develops and a space to think and feel opens up. We might talk through the process of labour or caesarean section. We talk about the baby, how the baby may look and feel, the understandable fearfulness parents may feel at the thought of seeing their baby, what they need to do around the baby. We talk about love and fear, we talk about love being their guide, their compass.

I am physically very present with them as people, I will hold them as they quake with emotions, I stroke their hair, I croon those mother sounds, catch their tears, I cajole them into eating and drinking. I advocate for them, negotiate for them, gently lead them to a place where their own 'knowing' of what they need to do for themselves and their baby can unfold.

To hold your own dead child in your arms is the most intimate and stark of experiences. All the senses are engaged, the touch of the baby's skin, the silkiness of the baby's hair, the intoxicating baby's smell, the weight of a small foot held in the palm of the hand- all the characteristics of the baby that mark its uniqueness, its individuality.

I have seen parents transformed time and again by the loveliness of their baby, even the most damaged, abnormal or tiny little baby. Amidst the distress of the baby's deadness, I see the claiming of the baby as baby, as their baby. I watch them trace with unsteady fingers the outline and contours of their baby's face and body, committing it to memory, much deeper and more profound and photographic image I might take.

Over time we talk about parting with the baby's body and together we will nestle the baby in the casket in preparation for his or her burial or cremation. Some families may choose to take their baby home overnight. We plan the rituals around remembering and fare welling the baby. We may talk about the legacy of the life unlived.

As we go on talking, we talk about the WHY of the baby's death, why them, why their little baby, why any baby? We talk about the baby having gone without them, to who knows where and what a total disruption to the natural order of life it is that this little baby should die before its parents. **The knowledge that death is not reserved for the ill or the elderly strikes a brutal truth for many.**

Many times, when people learning of my work, people will wonder at the sadness and weightiness of such a role. How can I describe for them the power of love at such times? To stand with people at the darkest of times, bearing witness to the outpouring of their grief and love for their baby, balances the burden of sadness I might bear.

It is about the mystery of life and death in life. It is about the power of love and ties that bind and endure. It is about and vulnerability that parents all over the world and all over time feel for their children. It is what makes us Human."

Personal Story

After experiencing the trauma of a stillbirth, Lemara worried about what would happen during her next pregnancy.

During my first pregnancy I was diagnosed with severe IUGR and our baby Robyn weighed a tiny 195g at 23 weeks. Unfortunately, there was nothing the doctors could do to save my pregnancy.

When it was time to deliver Robyn, I was admitted to a special bereavement suite away from other mothers and babies. My room for the night was designed to be more homely and my partner Jon was allowed to stay with me. The staff were very sympathetic and I had a visit from the chaplain which I found helpful. Robyn received a blessing whilst she was in the chapel of rest. I was also given a bereavement pack from the baby loss charity Sands.

Jon and I went away for a few days soon after the birth which was a good way of avoiding people. I found comfort organising Robyn's funeral; designing the obituary and adding poems and passages. I forced myself to continue going out and really wanted things to go back to how they were before the pregnancy. I went to a few Sands sessions which helped me feel less isolated. I even went back to work at a primary school after just three and a half weeks albeit in a less demanding role.

Friends and family were sympathetic in the early weeks but many stopped mentioning Robyn after a few months which was around Christmas time and my grief felt worse.

We tried to block out the pregnancy – we were probably in the denial stage of grief - but as time went on, I found I was surrounded by triggers. Seeing other pregnant women, new babies, adverts on TV and even songs could really impact how I was feeling. Jon was the only person I could really talk to about Robyn although I also attended ten weeks of counselling which was a good release for my bottled-up thoughts and feelings.

Jon and I soon realised that we desperately wanted to be parents to another baby and planned to try a year on from the anniversary. The following year, almost to the date, I found out that I was pregnant again. I felt a rush of excitement and anxiety.

I was really worried that I'd have IUGR again. I worried my baby could be even smaller than Robyn and I was always anxious to hear the baby's heartbeat in scans.

This time round I was much more proactive with booking in scans and doctor's appointments and even went to London for private early scans and a second opinion about managing the pregnancy. I was determined to do everything I could to help my baby survive. I was more conscious of what I ate, drank lots of water, slept on my left, and did everything by the book. I know lots of mothers can just carry on as normal whilst pregnant but I felt like I had to be very cautious because of my past.

After blood tests it was found my PAPP-A levels were extremely low again. This indicated that my baby was either high risk for Down's syndrome or high risk for a low birth weight. I took a private Harmony blood test and was given the all clear of Down's syndrome. I was warned that my baby would be extremely small and literally told to pray to God for a miracle. I took heed of this and also made a decision to think as positively about my pregnancy as possible. I read a couple of books by rainbow baby mothers about how to get through a second pregnancy and I practiced mindfulness to try and ease my anxiety.

My interpretation of mindfulness was setting aside 30 minutes every evening to think about my baby, block out the worries and feel thankful for reaching the stage in pregnancy that I was at. I would count the kicks, listen to relaxing instrumental music and take ten deep breaths while saying a personal mantra: "My body will nourish my baby, my baby will grow strong and healthy."

When I reached 24 weeks, I felt relieved. I was given a fantastic new consultant who monitored me closely and told me that although my baby would not be full term, we had to keep the pregnancy going as long as possible. Although my baby wasn't putting on any weight, I was told that her organs were developing at a normal rate.

My main thought during the pregnancy was that I had to keep my baby alive. At 28 weeks whilst I was resting and counting kicks, I didn't feel any movement. I poked my baby and ate something sweet but still no movement so I took myself to hospital whilst Jon was at work. It crossed my mind that I might be wasting hospital time as it was around 10.00pm but I also knew it was important to get checked out. Thankfully my baby had a strong heart beat but my scare did prompt my consultant to increase my scans to twice a week, a mixture of growth scans and Doppler scans, which made me feel more reassured.

My contractions started that same week and I was admitted to hospital. Four days later, my baby was showing signs of stress and I had an emergency c-section booked in for the afternoon. I felt nervous but with both my mum and partner by my side I found the strength to go to the delivery suite.

Everyone was really friendly in the delivery suite. There was a team of NICU nurses for my baby and an anaesthetist kept me preoccupied talking about baby names. He said it would be likely that my baby would have a very weak cry and that we might not hear her, however minutes later we were all deafened by an enormously loud baby bellow.

Annmarie, my rainbow baby, made her grand entrance into the world and at that moment I felt in my heart that she was going to be ok. She was strong and having read how premature babies are whisked away upon arrival, I was shocked to have her brought over to me for kisses. There was even time for a quick photo, and then Annmarie was rushed away as expected. I felt so proud of her and I couldn't wait to see her again, although I knew I might need to be patient.

After my c-section I was closely monitored. Jon and I were ecstatic when our first visit to the NICU was organised. Annmarie slept peacefully in her incubator with all the tubes I had imagined; I was so happy to see my baby girl alive and surviving

Annmarie's weight was confirmed to be 2lb. She weighed less than predicted and was completely off the percentile chart. The NICU team told us that Annmarie's main goal would be to gain weight and stay healthy. I was strongly encouraged to express milk and it was further fortified to give Annmarie extra calories.

It was a different world in the NICU, Christmas was approaching but I felt completely detached from the outside world. I learned about premature babies through the Little Bliss magazine and the Bliss website and spent all my hours practising skin-to-skin with Annmarie. We had the usual worries of NICU parents and it was challenging leaving Annmarie at nights and expressing round the clock.

Finally, after seven weeks in NICU, Annmarie weighed 4lb which was double her birth size. She was breast feeding well which was a miracle and I couldn't thank the team enough. Annmarie and I spent Boxing Day and the day after together on a semi-support ward and as a result of her continued weight gain, we were discharged and sent home where we were able celebrate the New Year.

Annmarie is now three-years-old and a happy, energetic child. She is still very petite but as a typical IUGR child she acts her age not her size! I am forever proud of my daughter and grateful to all the antenatal and neonatal staff that I have met over the years and to all the team at Bliss. Whilst Annmarie was an infant the one baby group that I took her to was the Bliss baby group - Early Birds and Seedlings where I felt safe with like-minded mums who understood the life of a NICU parent.

If you are pregnant with your own rainbow baby, don't be afraid to ask for help from medical professionals. Be proactive. Hospitals are doing some amazing work and Bliss is a great place to learn about inspiring stories and what NICU is like before you get there. Take one day at a time and try to be positive that everything will be ok this time. Be gentle with yourself if you feel down and be proud when you have positive days.

To friends and family of someone having a rainbow baby, try to understand that although the mum will be happy and excited to have a new baby, they will most likely be feeling anxious until the day that they take their baby home (and even then, there may always be some grief and anxiety). The new baby is not a replacement but a wonderful and cherished much wanted addition to the family.

It has been a rollercoaster journey but we can't believe how far we've come and are looking forward to our future.

How to Cope with the Grief of Infant Loss

Contributed by Zawn Villines

The loss of a child is often considered to be the most painful, wrenching experience a person can have. The loss of an infant may be sudden and shocking or follow many months of neonatal intensive care unit (NICU) visits.

Losing a baby means the loss of dreams for the baby's future. Parents may feel they were robbed of time to get to know their child. Friends and family may never have met the child. Because infant loss follows a short life, some people find loved ones treat the loss as if it were a miscarriage—not the loss of a living, breathing child. This can compound the pain and increase stigma.

Though infant loss is often painful and traumatic, it's possible to find healthy ways to cope. The right therapist can help parents find ways to mourn and honour their child. Therapy is not about forgetting the child or the loss; instead, the goal is to work through the pain of infant loss, move forward, and find ways to seek support from loved ones. Though life may never be the same, a good life is still possible.

HOW INFANT LOSS AFFECTS FAMILIES

The loss of any child is painful, and there is no good time to lose a child. The loss of an infant presents unique challenges and sources of grief. Some common issues include:

- **Getting loved ones to understand the magnitude of the loss.** Because the child was around for only a short period, some parents find loved ones treat the loss as if it were a miscarriage, not the death of a child.

- **Recovering from trauma surrounding the loss.** Many infants die following traumatic births or long NICU stays. Some die of sudden infant death syndrome (SIDS). In addition to grief, many parents feel exhausted by the trauma they faced leading up to or immediately following the baby's death.

- **Stigma.** The loss of a baby can be frightening to others, who may look for reasons it won't happen to them. For example, a pregnant family member might blame the death of a new born on a mother's habits while pregnant. This stigma can lead to feelings of anger, isolation, and guilt.

- **Self-loathing.** SIDS and accidental injuries, such as falls, are leading causes of infant death. Parents whose children die of these causes may feel guilty or endlessly second-guess themselves, which can trigger immense self-loathing.

- **Family trauma.** The loss of a baby affects an entire family. Siblings may not know how to process the loss, and parents may feel too overwhelmed by the loss to help their other children cope.

- **Relationship difficulties.** Parents who have lost a child may struggle to support each other, and sometimes, desperate to understand the loss, they blame one another. Divorce rates are higher among parents who have lost a child.

- **Physical challenges.** The death of a baby often follows a difficult pregnancy or labour. The mother may suffer injuries along with the baby. Coping with this loss while recovering from these injuries and managing postpartum changes can be challenging.

The loss of a baby can be frightening to others, who may look for reasons it won't happen to them.

STIGMA, MYTHS, AND OTHER CHALLENGES OF INFANT LOSS

The loss of a baby is tragic enough, yet many families also face stigma and other myths surrounding their loss. Some people mistakenly believe one baby can replace another, so they reassure the parents that they are lucky to already have children or that they'll one day be able to have another baby. This can undermine the meaning of the baby's life as a unique individual and may make bereavement worse.

Some other common challenges include:

- **Secrecy and stigma.** When an older child dies, family members and friends have gotten to meet the child and spend time with them. When an infant die, many people never get to know the child. Loved ones might not know how to talk about the loss and so may ignore it. This can cause parents to feel stigmatized or that they must process their grief in secret without support.

- **Confusion about infant loss.** Miscarriage, while tragic in its own right, is not the same as the loss of a baby. No matter how young the baby was when they died, losing a baby is losing a child, not a pregnancy.

- **Barriers to bonding with the baby.** Pregnancy complications and genetic defects are leading causes of infant loss. Many babies who die spend much of their lives in the NICU. In some cases, a parent might never get to take their child home from the hospital. Some parents never even get to hold their baby. This can complicate grief by making a parent feel that they didn't get to bond with or comfort the baby.

HOW TO HELP SOMEONE COPING WITH THE LOSS OF A BABY

There's no cure for the loss of a baby, and nothing can make the pain disappear. Grief in response to this type of loss is normal and understandable, so loved ones should not try to rush the grieving process or encourage parents to "move on." While it is possible to recover, parents will never forget their baby. Encouraging them to do otherwise is harmful.

Some strategies to help someone who has lost a baby include:

- Encourage your loved one to talk about the baby. Acknowledge the loss rather than hiding from it. Talk about the baby using their name.
- Talk about the baby at milestones, such as the baby's birthday and holidays.
- Find a way to celebrate the baby's life with their parents. For instance, help them plan a memorial service or donate to a child welfare charity in the name of the baby.
- Talk about how the baby affected your life if you met the baby. Even new-borns have personalities. The baby's smile, gentle demeanour, or desire to cuddle are all things to highlight.
- Never tell the parents another baby will replace the loss. Don't compare the death of a baby to a miscarriage.
- Offer material support in the months following the loss. Bring meals, offer childcare for other children, or help clean the house. Don't expect anything in return.
- Encourage other loved ones to talk about and honour the baby. If some family members are not particularly sensitive to the loss, act as a buffer.

- Be sensitive to the physical challenges of recovering from childbirth, especially if the pregnancy was difficult. Help the mother take care of her body by driving her to doctor's appointments or going to yoga together.
- Consider helping your loved one find a support group. Being with others who have faced a similar loss can be comforting.

Offer material support in the months following the loss. Bring meals, offer childcare for other children, or help clean the house.

THERAPY FOR INFANT LOSS

Therapy can help parents find productive ways to deal with their loss. Some therapists specialize in bereavement therapy that helps parents understand their emotions, work through the loss of their child, and even find meaning in the loss. For some people, the loss of a baby inspires them to support other parents, fight childhood illnesses, or otherwise give back to their community. Therapy can help parents decide what might help them move forward.

Therapy can also help family members and couples support each other. Everyone deals with loss differently. One spouse might want time alone, while the other might need a distraction or lots of hugs. Family and couples counselling can help with identifying these needs and support families to meet one another's needs.

Therapists gently guide bereaved families through their grief, and a good therapist never tells families to get over the loss. Instead, therapists honour the life of the lost baby while helping grieving parents continue to lead lives of meaning and purpose. Recovery is difficult, but possible.

References:

1. For family and friends–how to give support after a stillbirth. (n.d.). Retrieved from https://www.tommys.org/pregnancy-information/pregnancy-complications/pregnancy-loss/stillbirth/family-and-friends—how-give-support-after-stillbirth

2. Lyngstad, T. H. (2013). Bereavement and divorce: Does the death of a child affect parents' marital stability? *Family Science, 1*(4), 79-86. doi: 10.1080/19424620.2013.821762

3. What causes infant mortality? (2016, December 1). Retrieved from https://www.nichd.nih.gov/health/topics/infant-mortality/topicinfo/causes

4.

How Relationships Cope with the Death of a Premature Baby

Contributed by Jolyn Wells-Moran, PhD, MSW

According to a new research study, couples who lose a premature baby and communicate their personal grief with each other fare better than couples who don't. The researchers indicate that couples who don't communicate with each other about their bereavement frequently believe that the other person cares less or not all. They point out that women are generally more communicative about their sadness than men. This may mean that the female partner believes her male partner doesn't care or cares less than she does.

Surprising to the researchers, though, was that the male

partners in the study were more often in a deeper state of grief than their female partners. The researchers also said that the couples who communicated their grief with each other, called concordant grief, experienced what is referred to as significant post-traumatic growth in their relationships; more intimacy and even better communication.

The study was small, with just 22 couples involved, cross-sectional and all variables were evaluated at a single point in time – two to six years after the loss. Camille Wortman, Ph.D., a professor of social and health psychology at Stony Brook University, is quoted in an article in The Medical News, as saying, "It is not possible to infer causality from such a design" (April 22, 2009). She makes a good point, but the researchers may be on to what appears to be at least one conclusion that seems reasonable: Couples who don't share their grief might well have misunderstandings about what the other is feeling and this, in turn, could cause problems within the marriage.

The primary researcher, Stefan Büchi, M.D of University Hospital in Zurich was also quoted in The Medical News, encouraging couples who've lost a baby and haven't shared their grief with each other to seek professional help.

References

Büchi, S., Mörgeli, H., Schnyder, U., Jenewein, J., Glaser, A., Faucheré, J-C., Bucher, H. U., Sensky, T. Shared or discordant grief in couples 2-6 years after the death of their premature baby: effects on suffering and posttraumatic growth. Psychosomatics 50(2), 2008.

The Medical News. Couples cope in different ways following death of premature baby, April 22, 2009,

Men, Too, Deserve to Grieve the Loss of Their Babies

Contributed by: Emily Long, LPC

Miscarriage, stillbirth, and infant loss happen to men, too. Unfortunately, this reality isn't well recognized or acknowledged.

Instead, men are typically asked how their partners are handling things. If there's anything we can do to help or support her, they'll say, please just ask. Seemingly rarely are fathers of miscarriage, stillbirth, and infant loss asked how they, personally, are doing, or if they need support.

The assumption seems to be that since men don't carry the baby or experience of physical aspects of childbirth (and even miscarriage is a childbirth), they don't have the same relationship with the baby or experience the grief that women do when the baby dies. Perhaps in some circumstances—for some men—this is true, but my experience has taught me that, overwhelmingly, this is not the case.

Men grieve, too. They just aren't given the permission to grieve in the way that women are for such losses. Rather, men are expected (and frequently told) to "be strong" for their partners and to take care of everything so that their partners can grieve and heal. Even if they aren't outright told these things, the cultural expectation is so strong that often these fathers don't feel that they can ask for support or express their pain and loss to those around them.

Too often, constrained by family or cultural expectations, men push their grief away and attempt to rationalize their way through the experience. This doesn't take the grief away, though, and it doesn't help them to heal. Instead, their grief may begin to show up as anger toward and distance from their partner and loved ones.

Expecting these fathers to shoulder the burden of their partners' grief and healing without also providing them the support and space to express their grief is damaging and painful to them and those around them. These fathers deserve better from all of us — family, friends, and professionals.

Fathers of loss, I see you. This is what you deserve to hear:

Men grieve, too. They just aren't given the permission to grieve in the way that women are for such losses.

YOU LOST YOUR BABY, TOO

Your relationship with your baby might not have been the same as your partner's. You may not have carried your baby in your body, but this does not mean you didn't have a relationship with your baby and love him or her every bit as much as your partner. You also had dreams, ideas, and plans for your life with your baby. That was taken from you.

Perhaps you didn't physically experience the miscarriage, stillbirth, or birth of your baby, but you watched, hurting, as your partner went through it. Sometimes, having to watch someone you love in pain and being helpless to do anything about it is every bit as painful as the physical experience itself—especially when it seems everyone is expecting you to fix and handle things.

YOU HAVE THE RIGHT TO GRIEVE

This is your loss, too. You have every bit as much of a right and a need to grieve as your partner does.

You are allowed to break down. You are allowed to cry. You are allowed to be angry at the unfairness of it all. You are allowed to need time and space and people to lean on.

You lost your baby and all of your hopes and dreams for him

or her. You are allowed to grieve for all of that.

YOU ARE A FATHER—AND ALWAYS WILL BE

Your baby made your partner a mother and you a father. Nothing and no one can take that away from you. You are a father for the rest of your life.

You deserve to be included in Father's Day recognitions. You deserve to call yourself a dad. You deserve to be acknowledged as a father. You are one.

YOU HAVE THE RIGHT TO RECEIVE SUPPORT

You do not have to be the rock, the "strong" one, all the time. You deserve love and support from family and friends. You deserve to have your partner there for you as much as you are there for her.

What you and your partner are experiencing is one of the most devastating and painful losses that anyone can know. You cannot be the sole support and strength for your partner through it all, nor can she be for you. No one person can be everything for anyone. You both need and deserve love and support from others to make it through this.

You deserve to have friends and family to talk to about your loss. You deserve to have support from a counselor, a spiritual adviser if desired, and colleagues. You deserve to have people who can hold space for your grief, anger, and pain.

You do not have to do this alone.

How Children Grieve the Loss of a Sibling

Losing a child is a devastating and life-altering experience. Not only are the parents and extended family members of the deceased significantly affected by the loss, but siblings of the deceased are also dramatically impacted. When a child dies, the well-being of the parents is often everyone's primary concern, and it seems that few studies have looked at how children grieve the loss of a sibling. Understanding the coping strategies, they use and exploring their emotional state during the grieving process can provide an important contribution to the study of grieving.

Maru Barrera of the Department of Psychology, Haematology – Oncology Program at The Hospital for Sick Children and the Department of Public Health Sciences at the University of Toronto in Canada recently led a study looking at how children grieved the loss of a sibling to cancer. The data Barrera collected was gathered from parental reports and was based on children of all ages.

Several themes emerged from the study. First, Barrera found that although the death caused various reactions, the majority of the respondents were able to process their grief and continue on with life when assessed 18 months after the death. For young children who did not fully understand death at six months after the loss, they gained significant awareness about the permanence of death at the 18-month follow-up. Behaviour problems were not elevated in this group, but parents did note that these young children pretended to engage with their deceased sibling during play time, expressed concern for the well-being of their parents, and were able to verbalize their emotions of grief, sadness, and depression.

The older children and adolescents were less willing or able to verbalize their grief. The parents reported that these children acted out more and engaged in risk-taking behaviors that could be part of the normal developmental process of adolescence, but could also be attributed to their grief and loss. They did report adolescent children had more dreams of their siblings, wanted to be physically close to their siblings' possessions, and had aspirations to enter a field or dedicate their life's work in honor of their deceased siblings. Communication among parents and older children was strained and lacking, but again, Barrera is unsure whether this was due to the overwhelming grief of the parent and child, or was the result of the normal pulling away that occurs during adolescence. Overall, these results provide insight into the ways in which children of various ages process grief and adjust to the changes that the loss of a loved one creates. Barrera said, "Finally, these findings offer important guidance for the development of bereavement support services for this population."

Reference:

1. Barrera, Maru, Rifat Alam, Norma Mammone D'agostino, David B. Nicholas, and Gerald Schneiderman. Parental perceptions of siblings' grieving after a childhood cancer death: A longitudinal study. *Death Studies* 37.1 (2013): 25-46. Print.

Loss of a Teen

Helping Children and Teens Deal with Loss

Contributed by Marianne Esolen, L.M.S.W.

As a professional who has worked in one capacity or another with children and teens for nearly twenty years, the topic of grief and loss has been consistently present in all my interactions with young people. Long before I decided to return to graduate school for social work, I found myself encountering youth from all walks of life struggling to cope with issues of loss, from the grief attached to a parent's divorce to the grief associated with the death of a pet, friend, teacher, or parent. I found the topic in the hushed tones of colleagues, in groups for teen girls, acted out in games at a shelter for abused women, as quiet conversation among middle school students on a field trip, and as a random question or comment seemingly out of the blue during some recreational event, like a baseball game or Halloween Party. During most times when the topic emerged, there was a tentative and questioning look or brief and uneasy pause where I sensed a combination of hope and caution, curiosity and reservation.

For me as a young adult with a myriad of my own grief experiences (both those stemming from my childhood and those experienced as an adult), I recognized these occasions as both an opportunity and challenge. I would not be the adult who shifted uncomfortably in my seat, quickly changed the subject, nor would I be the adult who said all the textbook things while beginning to feel my body temperature rise under the stress. I would not be the adult who assumed the role of therapist and expert and forged ahead with a therapeutic treatment plan instead of a gentle conversation. What I determined with each interaction is that I would honour and accept the uniqueness of each child and their pace in grieving. I would continue to simply be me – warm, caring, intuitive, and always a listener. My stance, my calm, my willingness to allow children the space and time to deal in starts and stops with their grief, seemed always a surprise and relief to the young people I've met. Once given the permission and opportunity to discuss their losses, many of these young people had a lot to say, ask, wonder, and solve. And they always seem both surprised and relieved to be setting the tone and pace of the exploration.

As rewarding as the direct work with children has and continues to be, the broader goal of providing support and training to professionals in this area has been a personal mission for me. It became abundantly clear to me in my work with schools and youth agencies that one can have the correct letters before or after their name, be in an assigned role of a counsellor, and be uncomfortable dealing with this topic with children. Parents as well as professionals too can be bombarded with myths about children and grief that further breakdown the communication and build roadblocks instead of bridges toward understanding. It seems to me that if you can deal with this topic, you're obliged to dispel the myths, share your experiences, discover effective tools and activities, and increase the comfort and skill level of other adults, both professionals and the community at large. I subscribe to the belief Dr. Elizabeth Kubler-Ross shared with a reporter who asked her who was qualified to work with issues related to death and dying... "Anybody who loves to work with people and is compassionate, understanding, and willing to get rid of their own unfinished business. That is the only requirement."

I've shared that statement with every group, small or large, of adults I've spoken to on the topic of grief and children. It is indeed "the elephant in the room", a topic that makes most of us on some level uncomfortable and unsure of what to say or do. This discomfort seems only magnified when children are factored into the equation. What if I say the wrong thing? What if I say too much? What if they are too young to understand? What if I make them feel worse? What if they ask a question I can't answer? What if I don't know what to say at all? So many questions and yet I believe at the heart of all the questions and all the uneasiness is what Dr. Kubler Ross referred to as "unfinished business." You can know the textbook things to say, understand all the theories, and be unable to work with children who are grieving. In my experience it is a matter of learning to get comfortable with the elephant and learning to ride out the periods when you are uncomfortable as a possible bridge for continued personal and professional growth.

In this area as well as others, social workers, counsellors, teachers, adults in general must be acutely aware of their own feelings, beliefs, and thoughts related to death and dying. If this topic makes us uncomfortable, all the more reason we need to better comprehend the nature of grief and the value of supporting children. If we are to be helpful to those, we serve we must constantly look inward to recognize our own core beliefs, values, fears, and misconceptions. To work with grieving children is to embrace the losses we have already experienced as children and now as adults and to bravely meet those losses that inevitably await us on this brief stay on earth. One's attitudes and thoughts on the issue of death and dying greatly impact on the efficacy of the therapeutic relationship. The commitment to know thyself becomes paramount to this work and one's success.

We are first and foremost, human, long before we ever chose the profession of social work or counselling. I believe taking inventory, not once, but on a regular basis, of our experiences of loss as children and adults and our physical, emotional, mental, and spiritual responses, is a worthwhile process and one that only sharpens our ability to work effectively with children who are grieving. By thinking back to our childhood losses, we can reconnect with the perceptions and perspectives we had about death. We can also more easily identify our own fears and biases. It has been my experience that when dealing with children of all ages, honesty and empathy are the greatest communication builders. Sharing our humanity with children sets the stage for understanding and self-awareness, both are critical to a relationship of therapeutic integrity and authenticity.

In practical terms, this means a lot of self-reflection and internal exploration of those very grief experiences we've sustained. For many people this is an uncomfortable process but I believe short-circuiting this process will only interfere with one's efficacy with children. It is a complicated and highly charged emotional dance between a therapist and client. The process can become even more difficult if the professional is not aware or not dealing with unresolved grief issues. We can find ourselves inadvertently stifling communication or unknowingly displacing our feelings onto the child. Again, I say "know thyself." If it's uncomfortable then good – it should be – if you're never uncomfortable than it may be that you are not digging deep enough. For me it has always been a wake-up call to complete any activity I would bring to a group prior to that group. I've coloured, made collages, selected music, written letters, and completed many other tasks revisiting my own grief work again and again. Grief work then is all about getting comfortable with the elephant, taking time to remember the elephants in your own childhood and adulthood homes, and assuming the position of Companion in a child's grief journey. This article is merely a teaser, an invitation to reflect on the too often overlooked topic of grief, a chance to whet your appetite, consider your own experiences, and hopefully inspire you to continue your own education and professional development in the area of supporting grieving children.

How to Help a Teen Grieve the Loss of a Friend

Kathy Hardie-Williams, MEd, MS, NCC, LPC, LMFT, Parent Work Topic Expert Contributor

What does a counsellor say to a teen who just found out his or her best friend has died an unexpected death? I recently found myself facing that very challenge. I found myself asking, "What can I do or say to fill the space?"

Sometimes, there simply are no words. While adults often have strong opinions about what grief should look like, such as talking about feelings, teens often don't want to talk and just want to *be* with their feelings. An important lesson I learned is that when a teen is grieving, he/she needs to be given the same respect, trust, and space that adults receive when they are grieving in order to process feelings in his/her own way. Initially, teens often don't want to answer questions, do art therapy, journal about their feelings, etc.

As I sat with a teen in my office, wondering if I should implement the strategies stated above, I could almost hear the words, "Just let me have my feelings!" I began to realize that I was the one uncomfortable with the silence and with "just being there" as the teen tried to absorb and process an event that forever changed the teen's life. This is not to say that, at some point, opportunities for the teen to express grief won't be helpful and therapeutic; however, the process needs to happen on the teen's timeline, not mine.

There is no "right" way for teens to mourn the loss of a friend. I believe teens get through the mourning process in a more effective way if the adults in their lives walk that journey with them without trying to determine and/or tell them what they need and/or where they should be in the grieving process. Teens need to understand that they *are* in a grieving process and allow themselves to feel their feelings, which can be very scary. Initially, teens may resist allowing themselves to feel anger, sadness, confusion, the need for answers, and regret. They need to be given permission to "meet themselves where they are" and to understand that it is normal for their emotions to change frequently. At some point, opportunities for teens to express their grief through art, writing, talking, etc., will be helpful and therapeutic.

What is the best way for parents to "walk the journey" with a teen who has lost a friend to death? While each situation is different and individualized, parents can take the role of listener and learner and allow the teen to be the teacher. Parents need to follow their teen's lead. Another way parents can walk beside their teen without being intrusive is by providing the support of outside resources that the teen can access as he/she feels the need to or when he/she feels ready to, *before* the teen has an opportunity to get stuck in the grief process.

Parents need to be mindful of their own grief issues, as they will influence the way they relate to their teen. Parents often fear that their teen will become suicidal or stuck in their grief and believe they need to monitor the teen at all times. While this belief comes from a spirit of caring, sometimes a teen will feel smothered and become resentful if the teen perceives that he/she doesn't have the opportunity to grieve in his/her own way. While parents and other family members and friends should be nearby and available, a teen may need the opportunity to perceive that he/she has enough space to sob, yell, or scream without the fear that anyone can hear. Parents need to be careful of directing their teen's grief process as opposed to being a companion and support.

While teens should not be judged for the way they grieve, clearly there are constructive behaviors as well as destructive behaviors teens may engage in while mourning. Behaviors that are considered constructive are those that encourage teens to face their grief, such as talking with trusted family members or friends and expressing emotion (along with creating art, journaling, etc.). Behaviors that are considered destructive are those that allow teens to "numb" their feelings, such as drugs, alcohol, reckless sexual behaviour, antisocial behaviour, academic problems, etc.

Grief is not something that ends. Without the intention of being offensive, many often say, "You need to move on," but grief is not something one gets over. It is something that changes over time and is eventually accepted.

Loss of Parents

This is my favourite poem:

"You can shed tears that she is gone
Or you can smile because she has lived
You can close your eyes and pray that she'll come back
Or you can open your eyes and see all she's left
Your heart can be empty because you can't see her
Or you can be full of love you shared
You can turn your back on tomorrow and live yesterday
Or you can be happy for tomorrow because of yesterday
You can remember her and only that she is gone
Or you can cherish her memory and let it live on

You can cry and turn your mind,

Be empty and turn your back

Or can do what she'd want

Smile, open your eyes, love and go on."

Grieving the Loss of Your Parents

Contributed by Deb Del Vecchio-Scully, LPC, NCC, CMHS

The death of a parent is a loss like no other. Our relationships with our parents shape the fibre of who we are. Without them in our lives, a significant piece of our identity may irrevocably change. When unresolved feelings or even estrangement remains, the loss of one's parents can be even more complicated.

Becoming an adult orphan can be one of the hardest life transitions a person can experience. For me, the loss of my dad felt like the end of an era and the loss of my moral anchor. It was as if I had entered a new level of adulthood. A new path needed to be forged, and all of the familiar guideposts had suddenly shifted.

I often felt adrift and lost. My father's presence in my life was enormous, and in his absence I struggled to fill the void. I often felt anxious and afraid. Whom would I go to now for the unconditional love only my father could provide? Who could answer my questions about the past? I did not feel ready to be the keeper of the family wisdom; that was his job. Ready or not, in many cases the death of a parent forces you to assume a new role or responsibility within the family.

Losing your parents can cause you to question your identity.

One woman I work with in the therapy room whose father had recently died wondered aloud if she was still a daughter. The answer was and is yes, but in a different way. Our relationships with our parents live on in our hearts, minds, and memories.

Our parents live on in the way we honour their impact on our lives, traditions, and family rituals. For some adult orphans, the transition may mean the loss of a family home, mementos, and other treasured things. The responsibility to manage final tasks, as painful as they may be, can also be an important part of the mourning process.

Our parents live on in the way we honour their impact on our lives, traditions, and family rituals.

For many, losing our parents means losing a sense of safety and security. It may mean losing people—perhaps even the only people—who loved you unconditionally, who were your biggest supporters, and who occupied the greatest space in your life. Their presence in your life **may be matched only by their absence. The loss can feel overwhelming.**

Navigating this loss may take time, support, and patience. It may redefine your life and reshape it, perhaps even changing your priorities. You may find yourself suddenly more aware of the importance of documenting family gatherings and traditions. You may also have a deeper appreciation for the things that create these traditions, such as family photos, recipes for special occasions, or assembling holiday decorations.

There's no "right way" to cope with the loss of one's parents. However, the following suggestions and reminders can be helpful as you navigate this unfamiliar emotional landscape.

- **Be gentle with yourself.** The death of a parent is hard. If possible, give yourself as much time to grieve as needed without the additional stress of work or other life demands.

- **Pace yourself.** The tasks associated with arranging services, sorting through possessions, and handling the estate can be emotionally exhausting and simultaneously healing. Do what you can, focus on the things that must be done, ask for help when needed, and accept the support of loved ones and friends.
- **Prioritize rest and eating well.** Sleep might be difficult to come by, but without proper rest and nourishment, your body and mind cannot function well.
- **Make time for self-care.** Exercise and activities such as yoga or meditation can help manage the stress that comes with grief and loss.
- **Reach out to others who are also grieving.** Connect with other family members affected by the loss, or consider joining a local support group. The support of others who have recently experienced loss may help you feel less alone.
- **Use your loss to help others.** You may find comfort, for example, in donating a parent's clothing or belongings to charity.
- **Keep the past present.** Consider reinstating a tradition of your parents as a way to honor and remember them.

PERSONAL STORY
FATHER

Contributed by *Rafael Zoehler is a writer from São Paulo, Brazil.*

I had a father who was both firm and fun. Someone who

would tell a joke before grounding me. That way, I wouldn't feel so bad. Someone who kissed me on the forehead before I went to sleep. A habit which I passed on to my children. Someone who forced me to support the same football team he supported, and who explained things better than my mother. Do you know what I mean? A father like that is someone to be missed.

He never told me he was going to die. Even when he was lying on a hospital bed with tubes all over him, he didn't say a word. My father made plans for the next year even though he knew he wouldn't be around in the next month. Next year, we would go fishing, we would travel, we would visit places we've never been. Next year would be an amazing year. We lived the same dream.

> "I'm dead... So I wrote these letters for you. You must not open them before the right moment, OK? This is our deal." Love, Dad.
>
> I believe — actually I'm sure — he thought this should bring luck. He was a superstitious man. Thinking about the future was the way he found to keep hope alive. The bastard made me laugh until the very end. He knew about it. He didn't tell me. He didn't see me crying.

And suddenly, the next year was over before it even started.

My mother picked me up at school and we went to the hospital. The doctor told the news with all the sensitivity that doctors lose over the years. My mother cried. She did have a tiny bit of hope. As I said before, everyone does. I felt the blow. What does it mean? Wasn't it just a regular disease, the kind of disease doctors heal with a shot? I hated you, Dad. I felt betrayed. I screamed with anger in the hospital, until I realized my father was not around to ground me. I cried. Then, my father was once again a father to me. With a shoebox under her arm, a nurse came by to comfort me. The box was full of sealed envelopes, with sentences where the address should be. I couldn't understand exactly what was going on. The nurse then handed me a letter. The only letter that was out of the box.

"Your dad asked me to give you this letter. He spent the whole week writing these, and he wants you read it. Be strong." the nurse said, holding me.

The envelope read "WHEN I'M GONE." I opened it.

> Son,
>
> If you're reading this, I'm dead. I'm sorry. I knew I was going to die.
>
> I didn't want to tell you what was going to happen, I didn't want to see you crying. Well, it looks like I've made it. I think that a man who's about to die has the right to act a little bit selfish.
>
> Well, as you can see, I still have a lot to teach you. After all, you don't know crap about anything. So, I wrote these letters for you. You must not open them before the right moment, OK? This is our deal.
>
> I love you. Take care of your mom. You're the man of the house now.
>
> Love, Dad.
>
> PS: I didn't write letters to your mom. She's got my car.

He made me stop crying with his bad handwriting. Printing was not easy back then. His ugly writing, which I barely understood, made me feel calm. It made me smile. That's how my father did things. Like the joke before the grounding.

That box became the most important thing in the world for me. I told my mother not to open it. Those letters were mine and no one else could read them. I knew all the life moments written on the envelopes by heart. But it took a while for these moments to happen. And I forgot about it.

Seven years later, after we moved to a new place, I had no idea where I put the box. I couldn't remember it. And when we don't remember something, we usually don't care about it. If something goes lost in your memory, it doesn't mean you lost it. It simply doesn't exist anymore. It's like change in the pockets of your trousers.

"WHEN YOU LOSE YOUR VIRGINITY" came next in the pack, a letter I was hoping to open really soon.

And so, it happened. My teenage years and my mother's new boyfriend triggered what my father had anticipated a long time before. My mother had several boyfriends, and I always understood it. She never married again. I don't know why, but I like to believe that my father had been the love of her life. This boyfriend, however, was worthless. I thought she was humiliating herself by dating him. He had no respect for her. She deserved something a lot better than a guy she met at a bar.

I still remember the slap she gave me after I pronounced the word "bar." I'll admit that I deserved it. I learned that over the years. At the time, when my skin was still burning from the slap, I remembered the box and the letters. I remembered a specific letter, which read, "WHEN YOU HAVE THE WORST FIGHT EVER WITH YOUR MOM."

I ransacked my bedroom looking for it, which earned me another slap in the face. I found the box inside a suitcase lying on top of the wardrobe. The limbo. I looked through the letters, and realized that I had forgotten to open "WHEN YOU HAVE YOUR FIRST KISS." I hated myself for doing that, and I decided that would be the next letter I'd open. "WHEN YOU LOSE YOUR VIRGINITY" came next in the pack, a letter I was hoping to open really soon. Eventually I found what I was looking for.

> Now apologize to her.
>
> I don't know why you're fighting and I don't know who's

right. But I know your mother. So, a humble apology is the best way to get over this. I'm talking about a down-on-your-knees apology.

She's your mother, kid. She loves you more than anything in this world. Do you know that she went through natural birth because someone told her that it would be the best for you? Have you ever seen a woman giving birth? Do you need a bigger proof of love than that?

Apologize. She'll forgive you.

Love, Dad.

My father was not a great writer, he was just a bank clerk. But his words had a great impact on me. They were words that carried more wisdom than all of my 15 years of age at the time. (That wasn't very hard to achieve, though).

I rushed to my mother's room and opened the door. I was crying when she turned her head to look me in the eyes. She was also crying. I don't remember what she yelled at me. Probably something like "What do you want?" What I do remember is that I walked towards her holding the letter my father wrote. I held her in my arms, while my hands crumpled the old paper. She hugged me, and we both stood in silence.

My father's letter made her laugh a few minutes later. We made peace and talked a little about him. She told me about some of his most eccentric habits, such as eating salami with strawberries. Somehow, I felt he was sitting right next to us. Me, my mother, and a piece of my father, a piece he left for us, on a piece of paper. It felt good.

It didn't take long before I read "WHEN YOU LOSE YOUR VIRGINITY":

Congratulations, son.

Don't worry, it gets better with time. It always sucks the

first time. Mine happened with an ugly woman...who was also a prostitute.

My biggest fear is that you'd ask your mother what virginity is after reading what's on the letter. Or even worse, reading what I just wrote without knowing what jerking off is (you know what it is, right?). But that's none of my business.

Love, Dad.

My father followed me through my entire life. He was with me, even though he was not near me. His words did what no one else could: they gave me strength to overcome countless challenging moments in my life. He would always find a way to put a smile on my face when things looked grim, or clear my mind during those angry moments.

"WHEN YOU GET MARRIED" made me feel very emotional. But not so much as "WHEN YOU BECOME A FATHER." Now you'll understand what real love is, son. You'll realize how much you love her, but real love is something you'll feel for this little thing over there. I don't know if it's a boy or a girl. I'm just a corpse, I'm not a fortune teller.

Have fun. It's a great thing. Time is going to fly now, so make sure you'll be around. Never miss a moment, they never come back. Change diapers, bathe the baby, be a role model to this child. I think you have what it takes to be an amazing father, just like me.

The most painful letter I read in my entire life was also the shortest letter my father wrote. While he wrote those four words, I believe he suffered just as much as I did live through that moment. It took a while, but eventually I had to open "WHEN YOUR MOTHER IS GONE."

She is mine now.

A joke. A sad clown hiding his sadness with a smile on his makeup. It was the only letter that didn't make me smile, but I could see the reason.

I always kept the deal I had made with my father. I never read letters before their time. With the exception of "WHEN YOU REALIZE YOU'RE GAY." Since I never thought I'd have to open this one, I decided to read it. It was one of the funniest letters, by the way.

What can I say? I'm glad I'm dead.

Now, all joking aside, being half-dead made me realize that we care too much about things that don't matter much. Do you think that changes anything, son?

Don't be silly. Be happy.

I would always wait for the next moment, the next letter. The next lesson my father would teach me. It's amazing what a 27-year-old man can teach to an 85-year-old senior like me.

Now that I am lying on a hospital bed, with tubes in my nose and my throat thanks to this damn cancer, I run my fingers on the faded paper of the only letter I didn't open. The sentence "WHEN YOUR TIME COMES" is barely visible on the envelope. I don't want to open it. I'm scared. I don't want to believe that my time is near. It's a matter of hope, you know? No one believes they're going to die.

I take a deep breath, opening the envelope.

> Hello, son. I hope you're an old man now.
>
> You know, this letter was the easiest to write, and the first I wrote. It was the letter that set me free from the pain of losing you. I think your mind becomes clearer when you're this close to the end. It's easier to talk about it.
>
> In my last days here, I thought about the life I had. I had a brief life, but a very happy one. I was your father and the husband of your mother. What else could I ask for? It gave me peace of mind.

My advice for you: you don't have to be afraid

PS: I miss you

Losing Both Parents by Age 27: How I Began to Heal

Contributed by Lisa A. Snyder

I woke up to my dad staring blankly at the wall the morning of October 14, 2004. It was the day before my 23rd birthday. I knew this day was coming, but nothing would prepare me to wake up and find my dad no longer alive—just a lifeless shell. He had battled Hodgkin's lymphoma for a year and a half. At 54, his time here was over.

After my mom and I had cried over his body and walked the body bag down the hall, we decided to go out for lunch. Such an odd next step after your father was here on earth and now is suddenly just... not. We ate steak and potatoes and drank Diet Coke in his honor. It's these things, I'm pretty sure, that led him down the cancer path, but that's another story.

When I got home from lunch, I was all alone in the apartment we had lived in together. Strange things started happening. The lights went on and off. The song "Time Is Ticking Out" by The Cranberries was stuck on repeat on my stereo, the caps and numb locks on my keyboard blinked back and forth without me touching anything at all, and my quiet cat, Bastian, was staring up at the corner, meowing at the wall. I was sure this was my dad trying to communicate that he had crossed over.

When I looked at him earlier that day and had called out, "Dad?" as if he was going to respond to me... I knew he wasn't there, but what an odd thing? How can you be there and then... just not be there anymore? This moment made me come to be obsessed with learning about near-death experiences and worlds beyond the physical.

As I attempted to manoeuvre life, I felt like everyone started to disappear. The relationships my dad had built slowly started to fade. People were as scared to see or talk to me as I was of them, fearful of dealing with the harsh realities that my father was no longer with us. This took such a toll on my heart, as I wanted so badly to connect but had no idea how. How could life have brought me to this place of being 23 and not able to enjoy my dad in my life? Why do other people get this opportunity, yet it was "stolen" from me?

The Real Truth About Death

I continued to explore spirituality, reading many books about near-death experiences. P.M.H. Atwater changed my life with her book, *The Real Truth About Death*. In this book, Atwater tells the story of physically dying three times, each time going deeper into the afterlife. After returning from the dead, she interviewed more than 3,000 people from around the world who also had near-death experiences. After reading this book, I fully believed there was life after death. How could there not be? So many people from all over the world telling similar stories of tunnels, light, loved ones who had passed greeting them, and many times someone telling them their time is not over and it's time to go back... doctors who can verify that their heart stopped beating for long periods and they were thought to be totally dead... there are too many similarities from all walks of life, all religions and ages, not to believe.

One evening in September 2008, I had one of the most dramatic spiritual experiences of my existence. I remember this event very clearly because I was conscious for all of it. My father came to me as what I can only describe as a spiritual entity—a ball of energy and white light. I knew it was him because I could *feel* him. The last time I had felt him in that way, he was alive and here on earth. He told me, "You need to spend more time with your mom because you don't know how much longer she's going to be here." I took this information very seriously and decided to take the opportunity to have a big 27th birthday party and invite my mom.

The Red Party
In October 2008, I had a red-themed party. Everyone came dressed in their brightest red. It was so good to see my mom, as we were just beginning to become friends again after a long period of post-teenage-into-early-twenties angst and her not fully accepting me dating women (I'd like to note that on my dad's deathbed, he asked my mom to please accept me for who I am. Without the acceptance, we probably would not have a relationship in life.) This would be the last birthday she would spend with me.

A few days later, I learned that my uncle had taken my mom to the hospital. She was feeling weak and wanted to get checked out. I had planned to meet some new web clients at a cafe on this particular day. I'll never forget waiting for my clients to arrive and, in the meantime, getting the phone call from my mom. She never expressed too much sadness in my life, but on the other end of the line, she was crying. "Lisa, I have leukaemia," she said. My heart dropped into my stomach. I realized this could be the very moment my father tried to warn me about.

We started the cancer roller-coaster ride of deciding what chemo to get and hospital visits. A few months in, the doctors had told us she was officially in remission. Come to think of it, this may have been a lie my mom had told everyone so we wouldn't worry. In April 2009, her doctors had a sit-down with us and had the dreaded "there's nothing else we can do for you" conversation. "All of your inner organs have a tumour wrapped around them." ARE YOU SERIOUS? Part of me thought it was all a joke, and the other part of me was like, OK... OK universe... I know what's going to happen. You have prepared me for this once before, and I'm going to have to do this again.

"I'm Sorry You Won't Have Parents"
Later that day, I sat at my mother's feet as she placed herself in the Pepto Bismol-coloured recliner I had slept in many a night. She said, "I'm sorry you're not going to have any parents anymore." (This sentence has echoed in my brain thousands of times since this moment.) We used our time wisely, attempting to get things in order (or at least as in order as my mother would let them be). We watched our favourite movies, like "The Golden Child," and laughed and cried in each other's arms. I told her how much I was going to miss her... how much she meant to me, how thankful I was for her having me and everything she did for me in her life. She confided in me about things she would have never told a soul if she had the opportunity to continue on. We giggled at night about farts and stinky feet. I stopped my life to spend as much time with her as I could. I knew this time was precious and measured by the universe. I wasn't going to let one drop of it go.

I was with her during her last weeks on earth. As the day got closer, she began to see people. My dad and her mother had come to tell her it was soon time. She had also seen people in Bermuda shirts with red balloons getting ready to welcome her. She saw an angel and I asked her to describe her to me. Long, blonde hair, white light around her, beautiful white dress... I could tell my mom was readying herself to transition, and these greetings were comforting to her. I played Enya in the background. Got her a professional, cancer-trained masseuse. Asked friends to join us and play music. The dreaded coma before death finally began to set in, and I wasn't sure what moment she was going to go; it seemed like every breath could be her last.

Before I left to get some sleep, my mom had woken up with that last energy thrust many speak about (my dad had done the same). She was thirsty and hadn't had water in what felt like days. I had been wearing a special shirt just for my mom because she liked it. The last thing she ever said to me—and I have no idea how she could have even formed words, because she had been on the edge of death for so long—was, "That's a pretty shirt." Hours before she passed, I began to get blank emails sent from no one, with nowhere to reply to and no subject line. Friends came to spend last moments with her. Her body got cold, her temperature was no longer reading on a thermometer... and after midnight on June 23, 2009, I watched my mom take one last, long breath. I had been watching the heartbeat through her neck for hours; after the long sigh that came from her lips, there was no movement at all. She seemed to settle into a peaceful smile. Her brow had calmed... her last day on earth had finally come... and I realized all at once that I was actually, totally, and utterly alone.

I sat with her for a little while, until a crew of people came barrelling in to "place" her body so that when rigor mortis set in, she wasn't in a weird position. They told my uncle and me that we had about an hour and then had to leave, so we gathered up her things and walked out to the parking lot—which may have been even more weird than when I went out to lunch and then went home after my dad died. I told my uncle I loved him, went into my tired, blue jalopy, and cried harder than I had ever cried in my life. I wailed as the idea of being alone in the world sunk in... that I knew this day would come... but I was only 27 and would now have to live out the rest of my days attempting to make sense of being so young and without parents.

The days that followed were the most difficult in my life. Freshly moved by two beloved friends (I will never forget what you did for me) the day after my mom's funeral, one by one everyone I knew went back to their regularly scheduled lives and I was left in an empty apartment, with no parents and way too much alone time.

A Turning Point
During my mom's illness, I had started to paint whenever I came home from visiting her or when I felt sadness. Although I had gone to art school, I had never really done much work with the canvas. It gave me peace to move paint around with a brush... my fingers... a random object. It was something I felt was beautiful, that I could control, and that helped me express feelings that continued to bottle up. This was the creative outlet I needed.

For several years, friends had asked me to submit to a local community art show. I felt finally this was the year I was going to submit. I found this painting I had worked on during my mom's illness and decided to submit it to the show, completely releasing whether it would get bought and just focusing on the satisfaction of the simple act of submitting to a public show I'd always wanted to participate in.

I submitted it very last minute and the piece was placed in what I thought was a semi-punishing, badly lit area of the show. We spent hours at the show and, prior to our departure, my girlfriend and I stopped by for one more look—and there it was: a red dot! The piece had been sold!

Submitting this piece was a complete turning point for me. I learned that I had created a healing method that was between me and me. I could work through feelings by placing energy on the canvas, and suddenly I felt like negative energies such as fear and anxiety were being channelled and released on these canvases. The healing process had truly begun.

In April 2011, I decided I wanted to explore blogging. As a web designer, putting one together was easy, but what kind of writer was I? There was only one way to find out! I told myself that I would write when I felt pain and try to turn it into something positive, creating what has become a recipe book for myself and future life situations. My intention was to connect those who were suffering from parental loss, like I was, and to hopefully help myself and others heal through art, writing, and focusing on the positive. Thus, LosingYourParents.org was born.

My intention is to enjoy the time I have in this life, and if I'm not enjoying it, to figure out what I need to do to get unstuck. I got a tattoo that says "follow your bliss" to always remind me of this thing that can seem so easy to forget.

Using my blog and art has helped me tremendously through the healing process. Those of us who have lost our parents are forever changed and will never forget. I do have faith that if you're dedicated to wanting to live a brighter, lighter life, doing the work, finding the tools, and feeling the feelings will help you move forward. It has helped me. You've got to feel to heal.

Loving Myself: The Last and Best Lesson from My Dad

Contributed by Jennifer Martin

Here I am, three-and-a-half years after suddenly losing my dad when he was only 52 years old. Here I am. Here is this person, this woman, this wife, mother, daughter, granddaughter, sister, auntie, and friend. She stands tall, unbroken, stronger, healthier, and happy. Where I am now is a journey—sometimes a struggle—that continues on a daily basis.

I don't think you can understand fully the feelings of losing a parent unless you've lost one. The same goes for any loss; I don't think you can fully grasp the feeling until you've been through the exact same loss. For me; losing my dad immediately threw me into a whirlwind of taking care of everyone, on top of my own grieving. I took it all on, and after a year and a half, that took its toll on me, mentally and physically—so much so that I was hospitalized for a virus, extremely high blood pressure, palpitations, and stress. I was done. I was in a downward spiral, and my body was screaming and waving the white flag. It had surrendered.

After that, I made the conscious decision to end the madness. My dad was gone; he wasn't coming back. I was killing myself, and it all needed to stop. I am one person. I had to start putting myself first. I couldn't spend my life living in my mother's never-ending grief. I am a wife and mother, which are the most important roles in the world to me. What was I doing?

So, I ended it, just like that. I went to see my physician. I started exercising, walking, and doing yoga, and I did my first 5k. I started eating correctly. My mother and I attended a support group together for about a month. It really wasn't my "thing," so I started to write as my therapy. I started a blog and wrote my bleeding heart out. I started thinking differently. Writing helped me cope and move forward. My life took on new meaning. It wasn't overnight, and it wasn't easy, but my way of thinking and living changed. My views changed. I changed.

It feels like a long three years most of the time. It has been a long and hard journey that wasn't without sweat and tears. It came with highs and lows—it still does. It was a journey of physical successes and, most importantly, mental health wellness.

Grief can do many things to a person. You have to fight for your own life. You have to accept it. You have to deal with it in whatever way works best for you, because it will destroy you if you let it.

The things I have discovered about myself are amazing. The things that I have addressed, admitted, and apologized to myself for are accepted. I am 39 years old, and I finally feel like the person I want to be—the person I was meant to be. And I am free.

It's inconceivable to find positives in such a loss. It's not what is acceptable. I do wish my dad was here every single day of my life, but I have accepted that he isn't. His death has changed me and, in an indescribable way, has changed me as a person for the better.

It wasn't overnight, and it wasn't easy, but my way of thinking and living changed. My views changed. I changed.

I live life in the moment. I plan things, yet I am so spontaneous. I do things with my husband and children all the time. I've learned to let the house go, because sometimes there are more important things to do than clean the floor. I always spew my feelings, and I don't hold anything back. I don't let things eat at me; I can't. I NEVER leave things unsaid. I don't care what people think of me. I am not jealous. I will not beg someone to be my friend. I let things go. I will not tolerate liars or petty nonsense in my life. I say what I mean, and mean what I say. I am open. I take pictures of my children all the time. I capture almost all moments. I smile a lot. I forgive. I don't sweat the small stuff. I notice things now that I never thought much of, like sunsets or pretty skies. I am optimistic. I find the positive in most things. I don't want to wait to do things, like take trips or try new things. It's now; why wait? I am kind. I am not a fake; what you see is what you get. I am honest. I will not leave this earth with regrets. If I love you, you know it. I may disagree, but will respect the differences in opinion. I stll write now, it's like continuous therapy. I am thankful and appreciative.

There are so many things that have come to surface in my mind and in my life. Losing my dad so suddenly, and at his young age, has done nothing more than make me live in the moment. I know I am not guaranteed another day, but instead am lucky if I get one. I don't think there is anything he would rather see from the heavens above than for his family living life in the best possible way: healthy and happy.

I don't think there is necessarily a positive, per se, in losing my dad. But I sure have found meaning through it, which gives me such peace. I have been able to sort through my loss and become this stronger, different person. A person who felt cheated and lost, but who now has the ability to choose love over hate, understanding over anger, and belief over fear. That is what his death has come to mean to me, and I think he is/was beside me, showing me the way. The last and best gift he has given me is myself. I will always be grateful to him for that.

Helping Loved Ones Near the End of Life

Contributed by Tammy Black

My father's death in early 2011 of lung cancer brought about some unexpected gifts, hard though that experience was. And it was hard. Even though there's no way around the hard, someone recently told me that the right kind of support can make all the difference in how someone experiences the end of life. Truth be told, the right kind of support can make all the difference for everyone involved.

During his illness, my mother was, simply put, incredible. In general, our family does not express love by outward shows of loving kindness, sentimentality or even physical affection. It is our way, although that has changed some in the last decade or so.

Mama and Daddy loved each other very much, although true to our family nature, that affection was expressed via teasing and nudges as much as anything. When it was clear our time together was short, Mama became much more direct in her expressions of love and attention. She was tireless in how she took care of Daddy, understanding his needs and meeting them without any prompting. She stood by him, honouring his wishes and making sure he got what he needed in the very best way possible. She made sure he was able to die at home, being cared for by his family and a couple of nurses hired at the end to help support her as much as him. She loved him with all her body, mind, and soul during those last few weeks.

I'd never seen my parents so full of love, as paradoxical as that may sound. To see my mother cradling my father's head when he didn't feel good, to see her holding his face in her hands telling him that she/we loved him, to see her hold him to try to calm his shaking—it was amazing to watch, to hear, to feel. She was fully present with him the entire journey. It was powerful.

I say this not only as a daughter, but also as a therapist. I've seen the way people deal with extreme pain, grief, and trauma, and it's not always helpful, healthy, or selfless. People tend to try to avoid pain and loss in various ways, but Mom and Dad faced it together, fearlessly and courageously. It may sound trite, but I was so proud of them, especially her. Even though she was not sleeping and her life was being ripped out from under her, she stood firm and strong for him. Love truly prevailed.

And one of the best things about that is this: I know, absolutely and truly, that helped my father die with much peace and comfort. Love helped him transition on.

I'm not sure that my mother had a very clear idea of how she wanted things to be for my father, or, to be clearer, an articulated plan of how she wanted things to be. More importantly, she knew what my Dad wanted: to die at home (in his favourite recliner) surrounded by those who loved him and the land he loved. She took his cues, she responded with loving kindness, and she helped him live until he died. She was present and she listened, despite her own grief and pain.

How do we help loved ones who may be nearing the end of their lives? Show up. Listen. Respond. Feel, even if it hurts. Then show up, listen, respond, feel—even if it hurts. Repeat.

Am I Horrible for Not Crying at My Father's Funeral?

I recently attended my father's funeral, which was a very large gathering with family, friends, and people in the community. He touched many lives and was well-known around town, so hundreds of people showed up to pay respects. Tears were shed, handshakes and hugs were exchanged, and memories were shared. It was an emotional day, to say the least... but I didn't even come close to crying. In fact, I haven't cried at all since he passed. I've tried, because it seems like the thing to do, and because people have been telling me things like, "You just have to let it out," or, "You'll feel so much better afterward."

In general, I don't consider myself a very emotional person, though I've been known to shed a tear at sad movies. And I cried when my childhood dog died in my 20s. So it makes me feel even worse that I was able to express some emotion at those times and not now, at a clearly more impactful loss.

And it's not like I hated my dad, either. We'd grown apart in recent years, but I have positive memories from my childhood when my dad was around and not away for military service, as he often was.

My two siblings are grieving in "normal" ways, and they definitely think I'm some kind of monster for not crying at all, especially at the funeral. Meanwhile, I've been the one with a clear head on my shoulders to help our mother arrange the memorial, get her finances in order, etc. So at least some good has come out of my apathy. But I do wonder why I'm not reacting more strongly, and whether I should be doing something to make myself move through grief more.

Would it be helpful to try to make myself cry? Does crying *need* to be a part of grief? I don't want to draw the grief process out unnecessarily if I can instead just move forward.
—Dried Up

Professional's Reply

Dear Dried Up,

A parent's passing can be a momentous time in one's life—and assuming we know and outlive them, we all experience it eventually. Each of us will react in our own way. That means we will cry or not, feel sad or not, feel free or not, feel glad or not. Whatever our feelings or, more accurately, mixture of our feelings, we will be affected—some people more, some less, some more openly expressive, some less. That's all part of being human.

You dubbed yourself "Dried Up." I was surprised when I read that. What does it mean? Then I thought, "dried up" implies that what was wet before is dry now. I wonder if there were times in your early life when you were unhappy, and now you've reached equilibrium.

You write that you cried when your dog died and you also cry at certain movies. Some movies are arranged to make people cry; that's their purpose. And when your dog died, you were in your 20s, a time when people start truly becoming adults. Although I don't know you well enough to unravel what made you who you are, it's certainly possible your dog's death may have been associated with the end of your childhood. If so, you may have cried both for the dog and also that it marked the ending of a precious time in your life.

Now that your father has died, you wonder why you don't cry. You wonder if there is something wrong with you, perhaps. That presumes that crying is not only normal, but mandatory.

Who says you have to cry? Every person experience grief in their own way and in their own time. Everybody expresses their emotions differently, and there is no right way to do it.

Who says you have to cry? Every person experience grief in their own way and in their own time. Everybody expresses their emotions differently, and there is no right way to do it. It's a purely individual matter. You write that you are generally reserved emotionally—that's neither a positive nor a negative attribute, but rather a description of your place on a continuum of emotional expressiveness. Some people are more openly expressive, some less, just like some folks have brown eyes and others have blue eyes.

Your siblings seem to have precise ideas about the right and wrong ways to have feelings and subsequently show them. I wonder if this is not part of a larger story about how you relate to one another. They are not pleased with you because you did not display grief as they did. Do you all have to be the same? Is there only one way to be?

You speak of your apathy. I'm not sure I understand what you mean by that, and I wonder if you might mean impassivity rather than apathy, so I looked up apathy in the dictionary. Merriam-Webster differentiates apathy from impassivity:

"Impassivity stresses the absence of any external sign of emotion in action or facial expression." What's wrong with that?

I definitely do not think you should make yourself cry. You shouldn't make yourself do anything. Just be yourself and let things take their natural course.

How to Help Children Grieve the Death of a Parent

Kathy Hardie-Williams, MEd, MS, NCC, LPC, LMFT, Parent Work Topic Expert Contributor

From the time children are born, they count on their parents to provide a sense of safety as they learn about the complex world around them. When a parent dies, it may create intense emotional upheaval for children old enough to understand what has happened. Often, children do not know what to do with those feelings. Surviving parents, guardians, and other adults have a difficult task in helping such children process their grief and move forward.

Perhaps the most important thing anyone can offer a child who has lost a parent is time. Grief does not happen on a specific timetable, and the process of grieving may look very different from one child to the next.

In addition, adults can encourage children to share their feelings safely and without judgment. It is helpful to refrain from using words such as "should" or "should not" when talking to children about a loss or trauma they experienced. Adults can also facilitate a sense of togetherness or shared struggle to ensure children do not feel alone in their grief, and encourage compassion and support among other kids or people in the child's life.

The specific challenges facing children who have lost a parent include:

- Accepting the significance of the loss (it changes them forever)
- Allowing the grief process to unfold on their own terms as they work through painful feelings
- Transitioning into an environment where the parent is no longer physically present
- Maintaining a sense of connection with the lost parent while allowing themselves to live their life

Surviving parents have the unique challenge of providing support for their children as well as processing their own grief. Some parents may feel inclined to grieve in private, believing it is in the children's best interests to shield them from displays of pain. However, it is appropriate and healthy to allow children to see adults grieving because it signals that is okay to feel the impact of the loss and to openly express their own grief. The objective is to help children understand they are loved, supported, and far from alone in the grieving process.

Often one of the biggest challenges' children face when they lose a parent is to accept that they may be experiencing many different feelings. This is normal, and it's important for children to know that. It can be confusing when they feel emotions such as anger and yet miss their parent at the same time. Children may believe it's better not to show emotion and that if they don't, they may be able to forget about the parent they lost or forget the pain they feel. Caring adults need to let children know that when someone they love dies, it's important to remember them and cherish the positive memories they have.

It's important to help children understand that the goal is not to "get over" what happened, but to move toward

acceptance. They will never get over it; the loss of a parent changes a child from that point on.

It's important to help children understand that the goal is not to "get over" what happened, but to move toward acceptance. They will never get over it; the loss of a parent changes a child from that point on.

Adults often find it difficult to know what to say to children who have lost a parent. Others may be wary of bringing up difficult feelings in children or reopening emotional wounds. As a result, the topic may be avoided altogether, creating an "elephant in the room" effect and contributing to feelings of isolation.

The primary goals for caring adults in the lives of children who have lost a parent are to encourage them to accept their feelings rather than push them away and to offer support whenever it is needed. Often during the grief process, children will move back and forth through the various stages of grief. Being available to listen whenever they're ready to talk may be what is most comforting to them.

Ultimately, children need to know that there is no "right way" to get through the grief process. Everyone experiences it differently, and children should be encouraged not to judge themselves if the way they experience their grief is different from the way someone else does.

Loss of a Spouse/Partner

The death of a spouse is a devastating event, one that is met with both physical and psychological reactions. Even if the death of your spouse was expected, you go through a period of intense shock, grief, and loss. Often, your body manifests the physical symptoms of anxiety, depression or fear., it's important to take care of your physical and mental health after the death of a spouse

Increased Adrenaline

An increase in adrenaline is one of the characteristics of the "fight or flight" response to a crisis, and the loss of your spouse can provoke this type of panic This type of adrenaline spike can cause accelerated heartbeat; a tingling feeling in the fingers or lips; and involuntary shakiness of the limbs, hands or entire body. These symptoms can be very disturbing and uncomfortable to the sufferer and are difficult to resolve because there is no real physical "threat" to be confronted or avoided.

Exhaustion

Another common biological manifestation of grief and loss is physical exhaustion, reports Funeral Plan. Exhaustion may be the result either of insomnia, which is a very frequent occurrence among grieving spouses, or depression. You may find that you're sleeping too much and still very tired throughout the day. It may be that this symptom will pass, or you may benefit from an antidepressant medication.

- Another common biological manifestation of grief and loss is physical exhaustion, reports Funeral Plan.
- It may be that this symptom will pass, or you may benefit from an antidepressant medication.

Digestive Problems

The eating as well as other digestive problems can emerge after the death of a spouse. A lack of appetite is quite common among those adjusting to a loss, and you may also experience some problems digesting food you do manage to eat. Some of these digestive problems may include trouble swallowing due to a constricted oesophagus, nervous stomach, ulcers, vomiting, constipation or diarrhoea.

Emotional Numbness

One of the most common emotional effects of grief doesn't feel particularly "emotional" at all, reports Funeral Plan. Particularly in the beginning stages of grief, you may feel detached from your life, as though in a dreamlike state. This feeling results from the shock of your grief. The amount of time a person stays in this numb phase varies by individual. Your body and mind are reacting to protect you, since assimilating the full reality of your loss at once would be too painful.

- One of the most common emotional effects of grief doesn't feel particularly "emotional" at all, reports Funeral Plan.
- Your body and mind are reacting to protect you, since assimilating the full reality of your loss at once would be too painful.

Anger

Sadness is the most common emotion associated with death, but anger is another frequent feeling that is not often talked about. You may irrationally become angry at your spouse for "abandoning" you, or you may be angry with yourself for ways in which you disappointed your spouse in life. All of this is normal and natural, but if you find that you are having trouble getting past your feelings of anger, you may benefit from talking to a therapist.

Loss of a Spouse:
5 Things Only a Widow/er Understands

PERSONAL STORIES

Everything changes after the loss of a spouse or partner. For many, this was the person we spent most of our time with. This is who we made our plans with...the one who shared our worries. Every part of our past, present, and future revolved around this person, and to be without them is harder, sadder, and lonelier than we ever could have guessed.

And here's the thing...not only is it harder than we could have thought; the people we spend time don't always seem to recognize the depth and duration of this loss. This can be felt any time someone tries to cheer us up, smooth it over, or make it better. Our loved ones are well intentioned, there's no doubt, but here is what most grievers who have lost a spouse would want those around them to understand:

- **It's a couple's world and socializing after the loss of a spouse is never the same.** This comes up just about every time I facilitate a group for widow and widowers. We don't even notice how much of a couple's world it is until we're no longer part of it. Going out to dinner, going to the movies, taking a vacation. Sure, some people will do these things on their own, but for most these activities were reserved for their spouse or partner. And unfortunately, being part of a bigger group or going to a party isn't necessarily any easier. The problem isn't just the griever who may feel awkward in a setting that is mostly couples. The friends themselves may hesitate (or all out avoid) inviting the griever along for fear that this newly single person will feel out of place. And for most widows and widowers I speak to, nothing feels worse than that.

- **Even a very caring network of support can't replace this one thing we had: a shared and equally vested interest in the outcome of each other's lives.** A widow pointed this out to me, and boy was she right. "My friends are great," she said, "when I share a worry about my daughter or grandson, they'll nod and show compassion and concern. But here's the thing... in the end, whatever happens just won't affect them the same way it would affect me. The only person who could share the weight of these concerns was my husband". Since then, I've used this example. Imagine a restaurant opens. It's a wonderful restaurant, with a lot of loyal and happy customers. But then there's a fire, and suddenly the restaurant is no longer there. The patrons of that restaurant will miss eating there, and will feel saddened at its loss. But eventually, they will find another place to eat. The owner, however, will never be the same. Because every part of the owner's life and livelihood, and every part of their security and dreams and hopes went into that restaurant. And in the case of the loss of a spouse, the fact is that only our spouse or partner will feel the same investment and care in our life that we do.

- **Following the loss of a spouse or partner, I feel like only half of a whole.** A lot of couples will refer to their spouse or significant other as their "better half". While it's usually meant to be a sweet compliment, the truth is that most marriages (even the imperfect ones!) operate and function as two people joining their lives together as one. After the loss of a spouse most widows and widowers will report feeling that not only is their other half missing, but that they themselves feel incomplete. This union can become such a part of our identity that without it, we don't feel like a complete or whole person anymore. So, we're not only missing our spouse... we're missing ourselves too.

- **Every part of my day and routine is now changed and altered, especially when it's time to go to sleep**. There's no doubt that a parent who has lost a child, or a daughter who was the full-time caregiver for a parent will feel this same void and change in routine. But there are some differences with the loss of a spouse (and it's important to note that none of them are being highlighted to say that one type of loss is harder than another- they're just different). Household chores, sharing finances, making plans... all of these things can make it hard to get through the day after the loss of a spouse. But the promise of escape from these stresses that sleep may otherwise provide is something else a widow or widower may lose. Because unless a couple had already become accustomed to sleeping in separate beds (because of long term illness or nursing home placement, for example) a person who is dealing with the loss of a spouse or partner is going to be feeling this very significant change at the end of each day too. "Do I leave the light on the way he used to? I never liked it, but now it feels weird if I don't." "Do I stay on my side of the bed, or do I move to the middle?" "Even with the lights out and my eyes closed I can still feel the emptiness of the bed..." "How strange it feels to go to bed without having someone to say goodnight to- ending the day without a goodnight feels like leaving a period off a sentence"

- **My spouse/partner filled more than just one role in my life.** Losing even "just" one person in our life is hard enough. But following the loss of a spouse or partner, a griever will feel like they've lost many important people: their friend, their lover, their peer, their co-parent, their confidant, their business partner, their travel companion, their date...meaning that this loss doesn't mean the loss of "just" one person. This loss will create a vacancy in many roles that one very important person had previously filled. And no one person is going to be able to take the place of all the roles a spouse or partner filled.

- A list like this can be hard to create, but for the griever it can be even harder to read. So what is the point, really, in illustrating or highlighting all that a widow or widower has lost?

- I'll go back to the widow from the #2 point on our list, the woman who described the feeling of shared investment that she had lost when her husband died. She told me that the slow recognition of this fact was actually a huge turning point for her. Because when she started to take a look at all the reasons that she was struggling and all the reasons she missed her husband it revealed something even more important: all the things they had shared together. And lying underneath the sadness and yearning for what she had, was a realization of the blessings that their union and time together had created.

Val

2017

My husband and I had been together for almost 53 years and married for 50 of them when he was diagnosed with GBM4 in February 2017. He had been showing signs of not being very well for some months but despite previous scans they never found it until February and by then they gave him two months to live. He lived for four, most of them in a hospice, because after the diagnosis he went downhill very quickly. He was so brave, only thinking of us, mainly me and made me promise faithfully I would be ok. He died in my arms on the 15th June and my world fell apart. He was the love of my life, the only boyfriend I ever had and I really don't know how I have got through the last few months without him. I have amazing friends that have helped me and my son, daughter-in-law and three-year-old granddaughter, but of course they are grieving too, so much. My little princess does not know where her granddad has gone. We have explained but she is too young to understand, only that she misses him. Somehow in the first two months I managed to get myself out of bed and start the day, mainly down to my dog, who has to be looked after and was with us the moment my husband died, in fact it was him that woke at 5.30 a.m. because he sensed the time had come and had climbed on to the bed with my husband and was licking his face, trying to get some response. I also started a Facebook page and have run that for two weeks after he died, encouraging people, in a similar situation to myself to try and move forward in a positive way and that has helped me and them no end. As we can let off steam and get the reassurance that the feelings, we have been normal and have supported and encouraged each other through the hardest times. Only someone who has lost their live partner can possibly understand the grief and pain that accompanies it. At 73 I have lost friends and relatives to cancer and heart disease. I have lost beloved pets but this is like nothing else. It was always my worst nightmare to lose him but the reality is far worse than I could ever have envisaged. I am getting there, I am going out and actively seeking company and I can laugh and remember him with love, However, little things, like going for my flu jab today, on my own, will bring tears, or finding a little note with his writing. Or watching a television programme that is serialised and knowing that we watched it together and he is now not here. The emptiness is losing, the voice, the glances, the cuddles and the flutter in my stomach, that after all those years together still happened when he touched me or looked at me across a crowded room. You cannot replace that with memories or with anything else. I will make it, for him, for the courage he showed in those final months when he knew he was dying but never ceased to smile and make me happy. My heart goes out to everyone else on here who has lost their loved ones. It is a hard journey but it is possible.

Michelle

2018

My husband Chuck and I were married for 27 years – he went to work one day, and that afternoon I got a call from the hospital saying he collapsed at work and I needed to get to the hospital – they wouldn't tell me anything else. Of course I started running around in a circle not sure of what I was doing – called my nieces, sisters and friends – drove to the hospital and as I walked into the emergency room – I could see all of the people he worked with sitting there, but it was like they were statues that were just there looking at me – they took me to the back and told me a doctor would be in soon to take me to see my husband – wouldn't tell me anything else – I was freaking out – no one came – I finally walked into the hall and started calling out his name – they finally saw me and took me back into the room and told me he was gone – had a massive heart attack and they were not able to bring him back – I started screaming and they said, "You need to calm down!" Obviously they knew nothing about me and I thought – "Are you F.ing kidding me? Calm down – I don't think so". That moment and the rest play like a bad movie in mind head all the time. My husband died October 17th, 2017 – so it's been a little over 9 months and it is not getting any easier. Just like you – my husband was having some problems but his doctor said it was gas – and every time I asked him, he said – "Leave me alone – I' m fine." He would get so mad and storm off back to the bedroom – or wherever – I wasn't. Of course – now the guilt of should-have done this – should have made him go back to the Doctor – I feel so guilty because he always took care of me – Why didn't I take care of him and make him go back to the Doctor – maybe he would still be here with me? This all sucks – I cannot get past it – right after he passed was Thanksgiving and his Birthday – he would have been 57 years old – way too young. I think that hardest part for me about this is that I never got to say goodbye – I was not the one that was with him when he died. One of the worst parts of this whole thing was that he was supposed to walk our niece down the aisle 4 days later. My sister's daughter lived with us during the week while she finished High School in my area. My husband and I have no children – just dogs (our kids) and Chuck and my niece became so close – He was always good with all of our nieces – he had 5 girls to deal with – but he did a great job. In my heart, I know what happened – I could feel my little sister telling her and she was screaming so loud that the next door neighbours ran out thinking that someone was being killed or something – but I know that's what it felt like to her and it breaks my heart – it also kills me that my husband did not get to walk her down the aisle because he was so excited. I was on a Facebook video chat with my sister, nieces and their friends while they were trying on wedding dresses. They live about 45 minutes away from me and were going there early in the morning – I don't get up that early – so hence the video chat – anyway = Amanda put on the dress she was going to get and she looked absolutely beautiful – my husband was in the yard and I yelled to him to come and see something. I told him we were on a video chat with the girls at the Bridal Dress place – he said, "I think that's a girl thing" – I said whatever – he was standing behind me and Amanda walked back into the picture and he saw her – I could see in the screen that he was wiping tears from his cheek – he told her how beautiful she looked and he walked away. I thank God that he got to see her in her dress – the whole thing just kills me daily. – I think it's because it was so unexpected – you don't have the chance to get used to what is going to happen and didn't get to say goodbye – it really sucks. I can tell you – that my husband does send me messages – it was my birthday last week. The first one without him. I cried for a week before just thinking about it – My sisters, mom, aunt and friends kept me busy all day – plus of course my niece Amanda with her baby boy Blake – only thing that makes my heart smile anymore – we had gone to lunch and came back to my house to let Blake swim. My sister, best friend, Amanda and Blake and I were going to dinner after he swam. We went inside to get changed, my friend was in my bathroom – I walked back there – Amanda and my sister were still in the Kitchen. As I passed my hall bath, the smell of cologne was so strong. I walked into my bathroom and asked my friend, "Are you bathing in perfume" she said, "No I thought you had been back here spraying this" – The smell was so strong and, in that instance, – I recognized my husband's cologne – I almost knocked my friend down running to the kitchen to get my sister and niece. I said, "Hurry – come back to my room – quick" I was in front of them and as we passed the hall bath I turned to look back at my niece and sister – my Niece looked at me and smiled – she said, "OMG What!' We walked thru my room and on into the bathroom – it was like someone had taken a bottle of his cologne and thrown it all over the walls, ceiling, floor, – everywhere – my niece, sister and friend all started crying – my niece said, Aunt Michelle – you said last night you asked God to please let him come for your birthday- obviously – your prayer was answered – if he's not here – well he is here" I told my sister to look under the counter and make sure that his bottle of cologne had not been knocked over or something – she pulled it out and said, "No – it's closed tight" – Then we really started crying – the smell was overwhelming, and I could not believe it – it was even in the closet – I was so happy, but horribly sad at the same time. He has sent me other messages and I have told all of them about it, but I was really glad that they were all there as witnesses to see what happened. I told them that and they all say that they believe me when I tell them these crazy things that happen, but it's nice that they could really see it for themselves. I don't know if you talk to your husband – I'm sure you do, but I talk to mine all of the time – of course it starts out as a conversation and ends with me crying – I just cry every day – but I know for a fact that there is nothing – nothing anyone can say or do to fix it. I know it hurts my family that they cannot help me, but they all loved him so much – they understand. Everyone wants to help – doctors offer anti-depressants – but I tell them. No way – I am not going to wake up a year from now and say, "OMG my husband is dead" I am hitting this head on – head clear and do what I have to do – which sucks, but nothing else I can do. Told the guy that gives me Botox – "Don't think you have enough of that to fix my face!" So please – don't try to put any "I think I should do this because it's what you think people expect" Do what you feel – it you need to walk around crying – do it – if you need to talk to him – do it I got a heavy bag out and am going to hang it from a tree in my back yard and get my baseball bat and beat the s...t out of it when I start feeling this come one – I have been beating my fist on my granite counter top – but that hurts! So – I've got to slam my fists down or something – so I figure my heavy bag and a baseball bat will be the best thing. So again – whatever you need to do – you may not have to beat on a bag with a bat, but if it helps do it!

Lucy

2017

My husband, Bill, died unexpectedly from a blood clot. He was in hospital; legs were paralyzed from his prostate cancer spreading to the spine but it had stopped and he was actually doing pretty good considering. He got up in the morning and was in good spirits, chatting to his favourite nurse about a wood working project for our daughter, she had just turned 21 the day before. The nurse went out to get his breakfast tray and when she returned, he was unresponsive, they tried to revive him but he was gone. I got the phone call that he had died and I couldn't believe it. It's not like we didn't know he had been ill for quite a while. But both he and I seemed to have this problem with facing unpleasant realities in life. He was a compulsive debtor who ended up going through absolutely every dime we had, including having to sell our home...but I believe in him. I thought he could make his business successful. We would have been married 39 years this August. I didn't just rely upon him for everything, I was totally co-dependent. When we were bankrupted, I moved back to my family home, in with my mother, who has been widowed a long time and lives with my younger sister. It was devastating to lose a life time of savings, our home and my old lifestyle, which was quite affluent. I loved my husband and I thought by going along with him on everything was love. The smartest thing I did, while he was still alive, in this past year and a half was to join Al Anon because although he wasn't an alcoholic (my father was), he was a compulsive debtor and had the mindset of a gambler (thinking he'd get all the money back if he just landed the next big project). Joining Al Anon was a lifesaver for me. I would encourage anyone to seek out a 12 Step program and work it diligently. My husband died on April 6th and I too had to bury him on my birthday. I have a large family but none of my siblings helped out, they are all adult children of an alcoholic home, just like me, and none of them even know how it affected their lives – needless to say they are all drinkers. So, it was my Al Anon friends who were the support system that helped me through the funeral and it's my Al Anon friends who I go to now. I will be attending a bereavement group as well, mostly because I think it's wise to not be crying about my situation to others.

People start to avoid you because the bottom line, at least in my experience, is most of them are terrified of death. It's like if they hang around you, they'll catch it! So, spreading around the grief is a good idea. I would say I do my crying mostly alone and its then that I talk to my spouse and to God. Also, what I did is go onto YouTube and downloaded onto my iPod all sorts of meditations, visualizations and good talks on various subjects, but especially on loss and death. When my thoughts go negative, I put on my headphones and I listen to whatever appeals to me...this drowns out my own stinking thinking. I try to remind myself every day to pay attention to life, not death because God knows how long I have on this earth and I need to be grateful for my life too. I need to be a light for my daughter, she is dealing with the loss of the only father she has ever known and for her this is a second loss, since we adopted her at the age of 2 from an orphanage in eastern Europe where she was from birth until we met her. So, I have to live for her, for me and for the first time in 40 years since I'd been with my husband I have to work. So, there is a lot I have to live for...and although death has touched my life and it seems so awful and painful...there has to be another side to this experience that is not awful because everything in this world has its opposite. There are lessons to be learned if nothing else from death...and I am not ashamed to say that even as I read the eulogy I wrote for Bill at his burial, I felt a small twinge of gratitude...I thanked God I was alive. It was a beautiful, sunny warm day and it felt good to feel it on my face after another long cold Canadian winter. Another really helpful thing I am doing is to force my mind to stay present in this moment, read or look up Ekhart Tolle, who has made this concept famous. Living in the moment, that is to be focused only on this moment, not yesterday and not tomorrow, is the single biggest way I get through all of this...it's just one day at a time for me. So, when I step outside at 6:00 am as I did today, to drive my daughter to work, the first thing I notice, in the moment, is all the birds are singing. When I get out of the car, at night, and look up at the moon and the starts I remind myself that I am standing on a planet that is spinning in outer space, just one of trillions of galaxies. I marvel at the mysteries of life and convene with nature whenever I can...that is where I find my peace...just one moment at a time. If tears come up, then so be it, I cry not only for the man I loved and lost, but also out of sheer joy at being alive and being able to experience all of God's creation. Love and hugs to you all...remember, you are not alone.

Study Re-evaluates Factors of Resilience After Spouse Death

Contributed by Steven Pace

The death of a partner can be damaging to the mental and physical health of the survivor. Though previous research shows about 60% of people who lose a spouse have enough resilience to move forward and be satisfied with their lives, a new study suggests a majority of bereaved spouses may not be receiving the support they need.

According to the study, the traditional methods for evaluating readjustment following the death of a spouse fail to account for the many ways in which lives are impacted by the event. Mood, motivation, social behaviors, and sleeping habits are just a few of the areas of life that may suffer after loss.

Most evaluations of well-being after spousal loss only include self-reports of life satisfaction as the key measure, with symptoms of depression sometimes being monitored as well. But while many people report being satisfied with their lives, they may have difficulty in other areas that can affect overall quality of life.

The authors of this new study designed their experiment to identify the other factors that may help to understand the multidimensional nature of resilience.

EXPANDING THE DEFINITION OF RESILIENCE

Published online by the *Journal of Personality and Social Psychology*, this experiment took advantage of a database of information that was originally obtained in the Household Income and Labour Dynamics of Australia Study. In total, the researchers examined 13 consecutive years of responses from 421 people who had lost a spouse. Mathematical modelling was used to evaluate resilience by measuring life satisfaction along with emotional affect, general health, and physical functioning. The strongest predicting factors of positive resilience were also identified.

As measured by the traditional life-satisfaction variable, 66% of respondents reported positive resilience after the death of a spouse. When resilience was measured by changes in emotional tendencies, the findings showed only 19% eventually recovered from experiencing increased negative affect and just 26% reported a return to pre-loss levels of positive emotions.

Similarly, measures of resilience based on general health (37%) and physical functioning (28%) were significantly lower than the life-satisfaction result. The strongest predictors of positive recovery were the continuation of regular social interactions and feeling like a strong support system (family, friends, professionals) was available. The findings suggest a multidimensional approach to evaluating resilience after spousal death could be a better alternative to traditional measures.

ADDITIONAL RESEARCH ON RESILIENCE AFTER SPOUSE DEATH

Another recent study describes resilience after spousal death as a form of psychological adaptation that is reliant upon multiple factors. While the experiment focused on older people (ages 60-89) and would need additional data to evaluate other age groups, these findings also suggested recovery was related to several influences, including marital status, gender, and resilience as a personality trait.

References:

1. Brody, J. E. (2016, September 26). When a spouse dies, resilience can be uneven. Retrieved from http://www.nytimes.com/2016/09/27/well/family/when-a-spouse-dies-resilience-can-be-uneven.html?rref=collection/sectioncollection/health

2. Infurna, F. J., & Luthar, S. S. (2016). The multidimensional nature of resilience to spousal loss. *Journal of Personality and Social Psychology*. doi:10.1037/pspp0000095

3. Spahni, S., Bennett, K. M., & Perrig-Chiello, P. (2016). Psychological adaptation to spousal bereavement in old age: The role of trait resilience, marital history, and context of death. *Death Studies, 40*(3), 182-190. doi:10.1080/07481187.2015.110

Loss of a Friend

Still Worthy: Coping with Doubt and Grief After Loss

Contributed by Rose Stanek

Three years ago, my life changed overnight when I suddenly and very unexpectedly lost my best friend Diana. I can't begin to describe the shock I experienced, or the depth of pain and loss I felt.

I had made the decision to move home two weeks before this happened. The man I was dating at the time and I were in a long-distance relationship, and we had made the decision to move to Seattle together so we could continue to date seriously. However, I quickly learned that I felt estranged and completely isolated, almost like an alien living in a new world.

My world wasn't new, but it was no longer familiar to me. I would be surrounded by people having discussions about movies, their families, their hobbies, or their jobs, all conversations I would normally participate in, but all I could think about was the loss of my friend. My thoughts cycled: "Why did this happen? What plan does God have for me? Why did I have to lose her?"

My symptoms first started manifesting themselves physically, and painfully. I would experience intense nightmares, night terrors, and panic attacks. I couldn't control my emotions and was hypersensitive to everyone and everything. Sometimes I felt such pain, I thought my chest might literally split in two. I couldn't go on like this.

WORKING TO HEAL

When I couldn't bear it any longer, I finally committed myself to going to counselling. For two years I visited the same counsellor faithfully, keeping my appointment every week. It was in counselling I first learned about the power of self-care.

For me, self-care included better eating habits and exercise: I started eating more nutritiously and doing kickboxing every day. I lost 30 pounds, and I started to feel better. Little by little the pain subsided, until I was finally able to tune back in to my life. I felt happy, content, and peaceful and regained confidence in myself and in my life. When I thought of the future, I felt nothing but optimism for what might come. I felt like I was finally getting my life together after the challenges and pain I had experienced and the hard work I had done to overcome them.

But the worst part was yet to come.

NEW SETBACKS

When I was feeling at my best again, I began another romantic relationship with a friend I knew through a mutual friend in Utah, where I had lived before moving home to Seattle. As I'd long had feelings for this person, I was more than thrilled to be dating him. Things progressed, and eventually we became engaged. I was looking forward to our future, but then things started to unravel.

Although I had never been married, my fiancé had, and he was now divorced. As members of the LDS Church (The Church of Jesus Christ of Latter-Day Saints), we had to go through a process called a sealing clearance, since he was remarrying. I didn't know this process even existed until we tried to book the temple for our marriage, but it was standard procedure for remarriages.

A sealing clearance means the previous spouse writes a letter to the couple's ecclesiastical leader, disclosing any information that might have been undisclosed or hidden, such as <u>addiction</u> or <u>abuse</u>, and the church leaders review the letter and then either accept or deny the application to be sealed in the temple (married).

Our application was denied and then postponed for three months past our original wedding date. While I didn't mind waiting, I felt a great deal of uncertainty and <u>fear</u>. Why had it been denied? Finally I summoned my courage and was brave enough to ask to meet with my bishop.

The bishop was very concerned when we met, and we counselled for two hours. I won't disclose what he shared with me—no future bride wanted to hear the things I heard from him or experience what I felt upon hearing his words. But I had always looked up to the bishop and respected and trusted his perspective and wisdom. So, although I was heartbroken and confused, I decided to follow his counsel: I gave the ring my fiancée had given me back.

Even though I gave him back the ring, I truly didn't expect that would be the end of things. I thought, since we were partners who truly cared for each other, he would take the chance to work on himself and make changes so we could be married in the future. But he didn't. He simply left, saying "Rose, I always saw us as better friends than partners, anyway." The pain I felt that day eclipsed what I felt the day I lost Diana. I already knew how long and difficult the grieving process was, and so I knew the road ahead of me would not be easy. I accepted that pain, but I couldn't prepare myself fully for what would happen.

Three weeks after we ended things, my fiancée started dating someone else, a young woman I had actually confronted him about while we had been engaged. On occasion we would play games together at a friend's house, and I saw their interactions and felt in my gut that their behaviour toward each other was inappropriate. I asked him about her twice, but both times he denied having any feelings for her. Yet three months later, they were engaged, and their sealing clearance wasn't denied. Now they are expecting their first child.

This is my reality, but I do know today was slightly better than yesterday. Tomorrow might be better than today, and so on.

When I heard, I felt rage in a way I had not previously known existed. I felt robbed and completely betrayed—by him, by her, by God, by the whole world. Every time I got myself to a better place, I was knocked back down.

HOPE AMID LINGERING DOUBTS

My road has been a long and very difficult one. Some days I still can't understand how something like this could have happened. I was a good person. I had always been faithful. I always did my best, and I cared about people. Why wasn't that enough for God? Why wasn't that enough for my fiancée? But it has become easier to accept with time. The pain does subside, and now I have more clarity.

After the breaking of my engagement, I decided to start a business. I wanted to help people who were suffering just like I was. That business, however, combined with a precarious financial situation my fiancée left me in, put me into an additional $30,000 of debt, which led me to feel even greater shame.

So here I am, a year and a half later, still digging myself out of a financial, emotional, and spiritual hole that seems to have no bottom. I'm still paying off debt and living the repercussions of a decision that, despite being so flippantly made by him, has impacted me profoundly.

It takes strength and energy every day to combat the negative thoughts that relentlessly attack me. "You're unlovable." "Everyone you love leaves." "Everything you try fails." "God has it against you." "You'll never be successful." "Nothing you do matters." "You're 30, and look what you have to show for your life."

And so it goes, on and on. Some days it's hard to practice self-care, to face the challenges ahead. Whatever future I have feels tainted by a long-cast shadow of past disappointments and sorrow. In ways I've become more understanding, empathetic, and compassionate, but in other ways I've become jaded and untrusting. I still feel heartbroken, and I don't know if I'll ever be the happy, bubbly version of myself I once was, a woman who exuded optimism and opportunistic dreaming. I don't know if I'll be able to experience a day that isn't coloured by the consuming doubt in my mind.

This is my reality, but I do know today was slightly better than yesterday. Tomorrow might be better than today, and so on. I know I am still worthy of love; of the future I desire. I have hope that if I can rebuild my faith—my faith in myself, in God, in others—things will be bright once again.

Loss of Co-wor**ker**

Workplace Grief and Loss: By Blythe C. Landry, MEd, LCSW,

Most of us work for most of our lives. The relationships we develop through our work take up a lot of our time and emotional resources. Even though these are almost universal truths, we rarely consider the impact of grief and loss in the workplace.

There are many types of grief and loss that can occur in one's work environment. For the purposes of this article, I will offer tips on how to deal with the death of a co-worker.

Anytime a person dies, other people's lives are impacted. Most of the time, there is a direct impact on the people with whom they worked. Whether the deceased person worked at the local grocery store or was the CEO of a Fortune 500 company, someone they knew will struggle with the news.

Three tips for coping with grief and loss in the workplace:

1. BE CONSCIOUS AND CLEAR

When a colleague dies, it can rock the very foundation upon which the daily tasks of the workplace are built. Showing up to the office and having the person there one day and gone the next can be devastating.

As a society, we are taught to rationalize, avoid, or push pain away. We are taught that death is something we shouldn't talk about. These learned behaviours, while temporarily "useful" in avoiding pain, actually create shame, fear, and isolation around the loss.

Being conscious and clear about the death of your co-worker includes acknowledging the truth to yourself and others. It includes being a safe person with whom others can open up about their feelings and fears related to the loss. It involves consciously allowing yourself to personally grieve.

If you are a supervisor or manager, being conscious and clear means having an open-door policy in the days and weeks after the loss. It means being candid about the circumstances, as long as the desires of the person's family are respected. But it goes beyond that.

While the work must go on, honouring the emptiness is important. Pushing people right back into productivity mode without properly processing the loss as a unit may not only be detrimental to workplace culture, it may ultimately decrease productivity. Taking the time to work through it together is likely to build more trust and community.

2. ENCOURAGE FOCUSED FEELINGS

If you're a boss in an environment where someone has passed, it is your responsibility to facilitate support for employees. If the death was sudden and tragic (such as an accident or suicide), it is crucial that you hire a mental health professional to come in and be available. If the work environment is too small to have an employee assistance program (EAP) with grief support, there are professionals who offer private sessions and/or group counselling after a workplace loss.

If the loss wasn't unexpected (such as a long-term battle with cancer), your approach might be different. It might include an opportunity for your team to meet (either in or out of the office) to share stories about the colleague, or even a personalized office memorial.

While the work must go on, honouring the emptiness is important. Pushing people right back into productivity mode without properly processing the loss as a unit may not only be detrimental to workplace culture, it may ultimately decrease productivity.

Even though, for some of us, our co-workers can be our best friends, that doesn't mean there is crossover between office friendships and family connections. For this reason, I recommend office-focused memorialization. While attending a family-led memorial service might be healing, it may not be enough.

If an office-focused memorial isn't an option, other ideas for group processing include getting together at a local restaurant and sharing favourite memories; convening at a colleague's house and sharing a meal in the deceased person's honour; having a day where you all wear the person's favourite colour; or purchasing new office plants as a symbolic reminder that growth, despite the current pain, will eventually come.

These are just a few ideas to start with. You worked with the person. You knew them. Perhaps try a variation on any of these ideas that suits the spirit of your departed co-worker.

3. GET HELP

The most obvious thing many people think of when it comes to getting outside help is to hire an in-office therapist. Hiring an in-office therapist, especially for serious reactions and trauma related to grief and loss, is a great option, but it isn't the only one.

Perhaps you work in a place that doesn't allow for emotional processing. Maybe you work in a small operation where it's only you and the person who passed away. If your work environment doesn't offer support or isn't conducive to processing grief, consider finding your own therapist so you can safely work through your emotions.

Depending on where you live, there might be local support groups. Some of these groups are led by professionals, others by community members who experienced similar losses. Many of these groups are inexpensive; some are free.

Grief Multiplied

By Jade Wood
MA, LMFT, MHSA, Grief, Loss, and Bereavement

Experiencing grief and loss can have a profound effect on the way you experience your life, think about your future, and know yourself. It can be an intense and dismantling process, often running its own course on its own timeline. Because of this, individuals in mourning are rightly advised to be as loving toward themselves and practice as much self-care as possible.

However, it can be difficult to soothe yourself when you are constantly alerted to seemingly unstoppable news of horrible events taking place in the world. It can be especially overwhelming to experience personal loss juxtaposed with heart-breaking global tragedies. Grieving personal loss is challenging in itself and can push you to your edge; trying to simultaneously cope with upsetting events elsewhere in the world can easily seem like more than you can bear.

If the feeling that things are "all too much" is relatable and you find yourself especially sensitive to happenings around you, here are some things you can do to manage this trying time and the overwhelming emotions:

1. TRUST AND RESPECT YOUR PAIN LIMIT

Your mind and body will tell you how many emotions you can healthily hold. It will let you know when you have reached a point where your psyche is overwhelmed in a way that is not productive, healing, or good for your well-being.

Experiences such as anxiety; self-medicating with food, alcohol, or other means; disassociating through social media or television; forgetting things more easily; out-of-character experiences of irritability, hostility, and anger; and emotions that feel unpredictable, out of proportion, or explosive are cues that you have reached your emotional limit. These are your psyche's friendly warning signs—they may be unpleasant, but they are there to help you by alerting you that you are reaching maximum capacity. This means you need to take a step back, process, and discharge.

2. GIVE YOURSELF PERMISSION TO UNPLUG

It can feel wrong or cause guilt to stay away from news or world events, but it is critical you put your mental health first. The world is not going to be served by an informed yet emotionally spent or hysterical human, and taking in too much bad news may not be good for you.

Pain is informative, healing, and useful, and—like almost everything else in the world—too much of it can be destabilizing, damaging, and overall ineffectual. If you are experiencing grief, you already are carrying sorrow. You do not have to hold the weight of the world on your shoulders as well. You must take care of your own pain before you will be useful in supporting the pain of others.

3. PUT YOURSELF FIRST

You may often hear "put your oxygen mask on first" as an analogy to the credence of self-care. While it may seem trite, you have to take care of yourself in order to have the resilience you need to handle the present moment and navigate the future.

It can feel wrong or cause guilt to stay away from news or world events, but it is critical you put your mental health first.

Dealing with grief is loaded as is; when violence and sudden loss appear to be the norm in society, it is critical you prioritize your health. This means placing sleep at a premium, saying no to things which require energy you do not have, focusing on nutrition, and doing things that feel regenerating and empowering. Often, putting yourself first requires discipline. While at face value it may seem like a luxury (and it is), it requires saying no to other parts of yourself and to others, which can be triggering and difficult. Work with yourself on this, knowing your mental health and ability to remain grounded amid chaos makes all the difference.

4. FIND WAYS TO DISCHARGE

If you are carrying many emotions and experiences, you need to process them and most likely let them out. Therapy is an extremely useful vehicle for creating the space in which you can unload. Support groups are terrific for this as well.

Non-therapy activities—exercise/yoga, meditation, time in nature, dance—can also be therapeutic, so long as they allow you to process and serve as an outlet.

Events in the world can be frightening and intimidating, and it is normal to feel like your sense of control and safety is shattered. You may experience a heightened sense of fragility in yourself and those around you, and while this realization can be meaningful, it can also be devastating. Adding grief and personal loss into this equation can be a recipe for emotional burnout, high distress, and impaired functioning. In light of this, it is imperative you acknowledge that you are feeling dangerously overwhelmed, and then facilitate actions which reduce your stress and allow you to cope.

Suicide

Edited Version

It is time that we, as a society, openly talk about the severe impact of **Suicide** and mental health challenges. Suicide is a difficult topic for many people to discuss.

It is a fact that Suicide takes more lives every year than homicides do, and yet people rarely talk about the critical need to address this and other painful suicide statistics. Even though we have statistically analysed suicide deaths significantly, little has been done to reduce the risk of those who are particularly vulnerable.

There were 5691 suicides in England and Wales in 2019, with age-standardised rate of 11 deaths per 100,000 population.

Across all age groups, men aged 45 to 49 had the highest suicide rate at 25.5 deaths per 100,000, while the highest rate among women was 50-54 years-old at 7.4 deaths per 100,000. The suicide rate for women was also the highest since 2004.

Men accounted for around three-quarters of suicide deaths registered in 2019- 4303 compared with 1388 women. The male suicide rate of 16.9 deaths per 100,000 people was the highest since 2000. For women, the rate was 5.3 deaths per 100,000- the highest since 2004.

There are millions of people who are affected worldwide by the loss of a loved one from Suicide each year, and yet it is something that very few people still wish to talk about. Why is it that this killer is still so taboo? How do we want to stop the numbers from ever-increasing if we are not willing to have a real and thoughtful conversation about what leads to Suicide and the things that can be done, should be done, to prevent it?

Many people are talking about the experience of struggling with **suicidal thoughts** and the fight to keep them at bay. However, too often, the other victims of Suicide are forgotten. These are all of the people who are affected by death.

Depression and thoughts of Suicide are like a storm cloud that settles over you. All you see and feel is the darkness and intensity of the storm. When you're in the midst of the storm, you don't necessarily know that it will pass. You see darkness and feel hopelessness. When someone completes Suicide, they are doing it in part to end their darkness and hopelessness.

Suicide is a permanent solution to a problem that's typically temporary. And while it ends the concern for the one suffering, it creates myriad problems for survivors. In addition to grief and sadness, there is **anger, shame**, and **isolation**. We can talk about **cancer** and car accidents, but we don't know what to say when someone dies by his or her own hand.

To those who have loved someone who died by Suicide: I'm sorry.

It can be hard to understand because you look at some of the people who commit Suicide, and you think about how you always felt that they had everything going for them... and you wonder how you could have been so wrong about them.

Learning that a loved one has died by Suicide can be traumatic. In addition to all the feelings that anyone would feel about the death of a loved one, when the death is a suicide, there are additional feelings like:

- Extreme guilt for not preventing the Suicide
- Failure because a person they loved felt unloved and completed Suicide
- Anger or resentment at the person who chose to take his or her own life
- Confusion
- Distress over unresolved issues (many of which often exist in families where one person has a mental illness, which is common in people who die by Suicide)

How Suicide affects people

Dr Sidney Zisook, MD. professor of psychiatry, University of California, San Diego, told *Psychiatry Advisor*.

This section is intended to help you understand more about common reactions to bereavement by Suicide – physical and emotional – and how it can affect different people in the family and community.

We all respond differently to any sort of bereavement. We are individuals who each had a unique relationship with the person who died. There is no right or wrong way to feel.

When someone dies by Suicide, it reaches out across the community like ripples on a pond. Families and friends are devastated – and many more people are touched. You do not have to have had a family or personal relationship – the loss of an acquaintance, colleague, client or even a stranger can affect you.

A literature review comparing suicide-bereaved (SB) families to other bereaved groups found that SB families report higher levels of rejection, shame, stigma, the need to conceal the loved one's cause of death, and blaming.[3] Stigma may derive from a "societal perception that the act of suicide is a failure by the victim and the family to deal with some emotional issue."[4] Stigma and shame are barriers to seeking help and receiving support from mental health professionals as well as friends and family.[5]

Suicide is devastating, and the effects of Suicide on family members and loved ones of the person who has died by Suicide can be severe and far-reaching. Those left behind by Suicide are often known as suicide survivors, and while this is a tough position in which to find oneself, it is possible to heal and move forward.

Stigma and the Effects of Suicide in Family and Friends

When a person dies, societally, others generally offer empathy and compassion. Still, when a person dies by Suicide, there is a stigma around that death, and people often treat the loved ones of the person who committed Suicide differently. Loved ones can be petrified to talk about the Suicide for fear of judgment and condemnation – being blamed for the Suicide of their family member or friend. Because of this, one effect of Suicide on family and friends can be extreme isolation.

Guilt and Blame

Feelings of guilt often overlap with shame, compounding the sense of stigma. SB individuals often experience "intense guilt or feelings of responsibility for the death."[6]

Although self-blame can be present after any loss, it is more common after a suicidal loss, Dr Zisook observed. "There is a frequent feeling that you could or should have done something to prevent it, and guilt is prevalent."

Self-blame is one aspect of a broader tendency to find someone to blame for the Suicide, he noted.

"The survivor may blame the person who made a choice to die or may blame someone else who didn't do enough, didn't provide enough care, didn't return a phone call, missed important cues, had an argument or disappointed the person, or could have interrupted or prevented the death in some way. Or the survivor may blame the doctor for missing signals, not treating depression, or prescribing the wrong drug," Dr Zisook said.

Self-blame is particularly strong when the deceased is an individual's child.

"Losing any relative to suicide is traumatic, but there's probably no greater nightmare [than losing a child to suicide], since parents feel their job is to support their children, care for them, make them happy, and make their lives good, so suicide can make parents feel like a failure in this most important job of their lives," he commented.

Rumination and Anger

Rumination is common in SB individuals and is unique compared with bereaved individuals' responses to other losses, Dr Zisook pointed out.

"When someone dies of cancer, relatives do not typically wonder why the person died, while in suicide, survivors are plagued as to why the person did it — why, why, why," he said.

The Suicide sometimes comes as a "total shock" to the survivors, who may think, "He seemed to be doing better." "She had turned her life around." "He was making plans for the future."

Coupled with rumination are feelings of rejection and abandonment: "Why did she do this to me?" "Didn't he love me?" "How could she leave me?"

These feelings can lead to anger at the deceased,[6], which can compound the guilt.

If you are affected by Suicide in any way; The Following Helplines can help you

Need help?

Samaritans : 116 123. Website: **www.samaritans.org** . Email: jo@samaritans.org

Offer a 24-hour confidential helpline. You can also contact them by text or email.

NHS 111 Service : 111. Website: **www.nhs.uk** .

Call the NHS 111 service if you urgently require medical help or advice. The service is available 24-hours-a-day, 365-days-a-year. Calls are free from landlines and mobile phones.

Mind Infoline : 0300 123 3393. Website: **www.mind.org.uk** . Email: info@mind.org.uk. Text: 86463

Information on a range of mental health problems and support.

Lines are open 9am to 6pm, Monday to Friday (except for bank holidays).

HOPELineUK : 0800 068 41 41

A specialist telephone service staffed by trained professionals at PAPYRUS who give non-judgemental support, practical advice and information to children, teenagers, young adults aged up to 35 and anyone concerned about a young person. Opening hours are 10am to 10pm, Mondays to Fridays, 2pm to 5pm, weekends and bank holidays.

NSPCC Childline : 0800 1111. Website: **www.childline.org.uk**

Children's charity offering support and carrying out research into mental illness.

SANE : 0845 767 8000. Website: **www.sane.org.uk**

Email: sanemail@sane.org.uk

Out-of-hours mental health helpline offering specialist emotional support and information to anyone affected by mental illness, including family, friends and carers. Open every day from 6pm to 11pm.

CITIZEN'S ADVICE : Adviceline (England): 0800 144 8848. Advicelink (Wales): 0800 702 2020. Debt helpline: 0800 240 4420. Website: **www.citizensadvice.org.uk**

Professional help and advice on a range of problems, such as debt relief, benefits, housing and legal problems. Lines are available Monday to Friday, 9am to 5pm.

Understanding Suicide: 5 Myths about Suicide

It is time that we, as a society, openly talk about the severe impact of **Suicide** and mental health challenges. Suicide is a difficult topic for many people to discuss

The numbers behind Suicide are startling. Statistics show that nearly 6,000 people die from Suicide in the UK every year. The Centres for Disease Control and Prevention list it as the tenth leading cause of death in the UK. In fact, it can be estimated that a person dies from Suicide every two hours. One of the most discouraging facts about Suicide is that most people who attempt Suicide never **seek professional help** or care.

Deaths by Suicide do not just affect the person who ends his or her life. Suicide also has a negative impact on the friends, **family**, acquaintances, and community left behind. Effectively preventing Suicide is complicated and made more challenging by the stigma linked to it. However, improved awareness and understanding can reduce a largely preventable public severe health problem. Public attitudes must change, and we welcome others to **share their pain** and seek help when necessary.

In order to move forward in discussions and understanding about Suicide, it is helpful to dispel common myths about Suicide.

MYTHS ABOUT SUICIDE

1. Suicide is not a global issue.

This is simply not true. Only about 0.712% of suicides worldwide happen in England and Wales. Internationally, the World Health Organization estimates 800,000 dies by Suicide every year, equating to about one death from Suicide every 40 seconds. While some cultures, social groups, and ages have higher rates of Suicide, Suicide presents a problem across all **cultures**, **genders**, and ages. Many people passively think about Suicide at one point or another, as inner pain and suffering tend to weigh heavily on just about everyone at one time or another.

2. If someone fails at a suicide attempt, he or she will not try again.

Nearly 20% of people who die by Suicide have made at least one prior suicide attempt. Individuals that have attempted Suicide once are actually at greater risk of trying it again. Any suicidal thoughts or behaviors ought to be regarded as a serious concern—people who are feeling suicidal need immediate support to work toward a resolution. Therapy, sometimes in conjunction with **medication**, has proven effective in preventing multiple suicide attempts.

3. If someone has resolved to end their life, they cannot be stopped.

Most people thinking about Suicide do not want to die; they simply want to end the pain they are experiencing. Even though there are some instances where no one could have predicted a suicide, in most instances, if necessary, help and support are given to a person who is willing to accept the help, a tragic result may be prevented. Suicidal people can change their minds; therapy, encouragement, unconditional **love**, and psychiatric interventions can all help them on their path to recovery.

4. Asking someone if they feel suicidal can encourage suicide attempts.

Having a serious talk about Suicide with someone does not create or enhance the risk of death. Talking with someone about their suicidal ideation can help lower their risk. The most appropriate way of identifying the possibility of Suicide is to ask directly. Openly discussing and keenly listening to somebody's thoughts of Suicide can give them a source of relief and can be crucial in getting them help and preventing the immediate risk of Suicide.

5. People who talk about Suicide do not attempt or complete it.

People who talk about their suicidal thoughts may attempt Suicide in the future, so you mustn't dismiss any talk of Suicide by others. Most people who die by Suicide had confided in somebody in the days or weeks before their death. Listening, offering support, and assisting someone who is suicidal to get immediate professional help can save lives.

WHERE YOU CAN GET HELP

If you have suicidal thoughts, reach out to someone immediately. This can be a trusted friend, family member, religious leader, therapist, or doctor. If you do not have somebody to turn to, you can call the suicide prevention hotline in UK. **The contact details are provided below**. If you are outside the UK, visit suicide.org or IASP to get a helpline within your locality. You may also find help at:

- **stopasuicide.org** provides people with warning signs of Suicide so you can help prevent others from such an act.
- **suicidepreventionlifeline.org** allows people to call or chat online with a suicide prevention counsellor.
- **thetrevorproject.org** offers life-affirming programs to members of the LGBTQ youth community at Risk for Suicide, in the United Kingdom

If you feel you are in immediate danger to yourself or others, you can call your local law enforcement agency (dial 999 in UK) or go to the nearest emergency hospital room.

Working with a therapist or counsellor is a safe way to face emotional pain or talk about suicidal ideation.

References:

1. Fast Stats: Leading causes of death. (2014, July 14). *Centers for Disease Control and Prevention.* Retrieved August 20, 2014, from http://www.cdc.gov/nchs/fastats/leading-causes-of-death.htm

2. Key research findings. *American Foundation for Suicide Prevention*. Retrieved August 20, 2014, from https://www.afsp.org/understanding-suicide/key-research-findings

3. McIntosh, J. L., & Drapeau, C. W. (2014). U.S.A. Suicide: 2011 official final data. *American Association of Suicidology.* Retrieved August 18, 2014 from http://www.suicidology.org/Portals/14/docs/Resources/FactSheets/2011OverallData.pdf

4. Suicide facts. *Suicide Awareness Voices of Education.* Retrieved August 18, 2014, from http://www.save.org/index.cfm?fuseaction=home.viewPage&page_id=705D5DF4-055B-F1EC-3F66462866FCB4E6

5. Suicide prevention (SUPRE). (n.d.). *World Health Organization.* Retrieved August 22, 2014

Contributed Good Therapy.Org

When **Suicide** happens, it often staggers everyone left behind. Questions linger. Why would someone even consider Suicide? Why didn't they just **reach out for help**? Feelings of isolation, fear, uncertainty, anger, or disbelief are common. Understanding is less so.

For some of the people with whom I work in **therapy**, primarily **teens**, Suicide is sometimes viewed as a means to an end. It is seen as a way to end the pain they feel. It isn't always some "tiny voice" they think they hear telling them to end it all.

Suicidal thoughts serve as a symptom that something isn't right. For some, Suicide is the heart's and mind's way of searching for an answer to psychological and emotional agony.

When I do speak engagements or meet with families, I explain that Suicide isn't always the result of an "illness." You don't have to be ill, mentally, or otherwise, to consider Suicide. Suicide is sometimes seen merely as a tool by those who don't see a purpose in living. Why Suicide becomes, their tool of choice is harder to comprehend.

There is a considerable lack of awareness in our culture about the factors that may contribute to Suicide. That lack of awareness tends to leave us stunned when we hear about someone ending their own life, whether we knew the person or they were a celebrity. Sadly, the shock of Suicide that many of us experience when it occurs may stem from:

There is a considerable lack of awareness in our culture about the factors that may contribute to Suicide. That lack of awareness tends to leave us stunned when we hear about someone ending their own life, whether we knew the person or they were a celebrity.

- **The romanticized view of fame and talent:** We tend to fixate on sex appeal, fashion, money, and fame. It's no surprise, then, that society holds firmly to the view that if you are famous/attractive/talented/popular, you are without troubles. This belief keeps us limited in our view of why Suicide happens among the successful, wealthy, and famous.

- **Emphasis on mood and affect:** Many people assume that if someone is smiling and appearing to be in good spirits, they must be **happy** and satisfied with their life. The sad reality is we cannot rely solely on a person's **mood** and affect to determine their zeal for life. Mood and affect are powerful. They can get us jobs and dates. Because we had to learn to adjust our mindset and affect to fit daily life expectations, many people hide behind a mask of positivity to survive.

- **The narrow view of existential discomfort:** Most people can be assumed to believe there are many reasons to live and few reasons to die. But we must keep in mind that for some, dying seems far more attractive than living. We don't walk in anyone else's shoes, and we don't know how a person views life from day today. We are constantly changing.

- **Associating Suicide with mental illness:** Mental health is being talked about more than ever. While that has helped efforts to **destigmatize** mental health conditions and invited more **empathy**, people whose impressions of Suicide come primarily from the media may incorrectly associate it with mental health problems. For example, some may hypothesize that Anthony Bourdain's death resulted from an undetected or untreated **mental illness**. But we can also hypothesize that his Suicide may have been the result of an existential crisis that he internalized.

According to the World Health Organization, almost 800,000 people die by Suicide around the world each year. That equates to one person dying by Suicide every 40 seconds.

It's an epidemic. It's a tragedy. It's traumatic.

But it's not enough to understand how prevalent Suicide is. We need to adjust how we think about it and work to educate others. The deaths of famous people that seem to catch us by surprise should instead wake us up. Instead of letting that shocked feeling come and go, we should let it stimulate within us the courage to change.

Reference:

Suicide data. (n.d.). World Health Organization. Retrieved from
http://www.who.int/mental_health/prevention/suicide/suicide prevent/en

Child and Teen Suicide Attempts Nearly Doubled in 9 Years

The number of teenage suicides in **England** and **Wales** increased by 67 percent between 2010 and 2017.

Office of National Statistics (ONS) figures show that in the last year alone, 187 under 19s took their own lives, compared with 162 the year before - a rise of 15 percent.

At the start of the decade in 2010, the figure stood at 112. Since then, tuition fees have increased, while studies have linked social media to increasing anxiety and depression among teenagers.

The latest figures follow June's announcement that London's teenage suicide rate had increased at more than four times the national rate, rising by 107 percent in the three years from 2013 to 2016 – from 14 to 29.

Participants ranged from age 5 to age 17. Suicidal gestures increased across all age groups. The largest increase was among 15- to 17-year-olds, followed by children aged 12-14 years.

Girls saw larger increases in hospitalization than boys. Nearly two-thirds of children hospitalized for suicidal gestures were girls.

The study also uncovered seasonal swings in suicidal gestures. Rates of suicidality in youth were highest in spring and fall. The rates were lowest in summer, with just 18.5% of suicide attempts occurring between June and August. By contrast, the summer months have been linked to an increase in Suicide among adults.

WHAT'S BEHIND THE RISE IN SUICIDES?

The study did not directly assess risk factors for Suicide. Yet seasonal patterns in the data led the study authors to believe school was a large influence. They suggest increased **academic** and social pressures during the school year may factor into suicide risk.

Previous research has found an increase in **depression** in teens, especially teen girls. Depression can lead to Suicide if left untreated.

Two studies published earlier this year in Paediatrics explored risk factors for Suicide among teens. One study found a heightened risk of Suicide and **self-harm** among homeless teens. Another found that teens who self-harm are more likely to later attempt Suicide.

The risk of a subsequent suicide attempt is even higher among homeless teens who self-harm. The teens aged 12-17 years are more likely than adults to be homeless.

Research consistently finds higher rates of Suicide and suicidal thoughts among **marginalized** teens. There are unusually **high rates among transgender youth**.

Though many risk factors play a role in Suicide, **Suicide is preventable**. A trained **therapist** can help teens and children cope with overwhelming emotions, stress, depression, and anxiety. If you or someone you know; experiences suicidal thoughts or feelings, please get help.

How to Help Your Teen Process the Suicide of a Peer

By Katelyn Alcamo, LCMFT, GoodTherapy.org Topic Expert

Over the past couple of months, there has been a teen suicide at each of two neighbouring high schools in my community. To say this is tragic is an understatement. As a **child and adolescent** therapist, I knew these suicides were going to make their way into my therapy office during the following weeks. In fact, I was going to ensure they did because I am a firm believer it is important for therapists, and other adults, to talk with teens about **Suicide**. Why? Because teens are already talking about it, it is likely the people they are talking to are not knowledgeable about helping them process such an act healthily and helpfully.

When a teen in a community commits Suicide, there is a full spectrum of feelings among other teens. Teens may feel confused, **sad**, **angry**, curious, **anxious**, numb, or **scared**. Some may feel **triggered** and have their own thoughts about Suicide or **self-harm**. Some may be frustrated by the sudden outpouring of love and attention that the teen who died gets, especially if it feels disingenuous. And some may have a hard time processing what would bring a peer to decide to end their life. Regardless, these reactions often get a desire to talk about what happened. In seeking to understand, teens may turn to social media, including Instagram and Facebook pages that share unfiltered photos and information on Suicide and self-harm. These are not the places we want our children to be learning about such topics.

Talking with teens about Suicide is also essential because they are often the first line of defence in preventing teens from ending their lives. Most suicidal teens have expressed suicidal ideation, whether blatantly or subtly, to friends or peers either in person or via social media. Unfortunately, many teens don't know what to do with the information, are unsure of the signs to look out for, or don't want to be "that person" who snitches or gets involved.

Especially following the Suicide of an adolescent, there are things that adults can do to not only help teens process the loss but also help prevent other suicides. The first is to know and recognize the signs and symptoms of **depression** and suicidal ideation. Following a suicide, these signs and symptoms may be heightened in adolescents, especially in already depressed, anxious, or suicidal teens:

- Depressed or anxious mood
- Frequent running away
- Expressions of suicidal thoughts and talk of death
- Withdrawal from friends, family, and activities
- **Impulsive** and sometimes **aggressive** behaviour
- **Alcohol and drug abuse**
- Engaging in high-risk behaviors
- Social **isolation**
- Low **self-esteem**
- Giving away meaningful belongings
- Self-harm behaviour
- Suggestive social media messages, videos, posts

Equally important is how to take action and be a safety net for adolescents in need. As an adult, it is important to be available to adolescents and talk openly with them about Suicide. It is essential that adults check-in directly with teens following the Suicide of a peer, especially if there have been prior concerning signs or symptoms. Parents, teachers, and counsellors alike should process the loss with teens and explore how they are feeling, what they are thinking, and how they are coping with the loss. Some helpful questions include:

It can feel scary to talk about Suicide, but in my experience, it is important to speak directly with adolescents to help them deal with this topic. If you are unsure how to talk with your teen about Suicide, connect them with their guidance counsellor or a therapist who can help them process any feelings they might be having.

- How well did you know the teen who died?
- How do you feel about the news?
- What are some thoughts or questions you have been having since hearing about it?
- Have you talked to anyone about the Suicide?
- Have you seen any information online about Suicide?
- How has your school (whether it is the school that the person who died attended or not) addressed the Suicide?
- Have you ever thought about killing or hurting yourself? What can you do or who can you talk to if you have those thoughts?
- Do you know anyone who has expressed those thoughts/feelings? How have you handled that? How do you feel about that?
- What can you do if you hear that someone has suicidal thoughts?

After exploring some of these questions, it is important to help them develop a plan for what they can do if they have a concern for a peer and explore any potential resistance. It can help communicate that there are ways to report their concerns in a confidential way that can protect their relationship with the peer. Emphasize the importance of doing something.

It is also important to help them identify their own coping strategies to manage things such as anxiety, depression, peer problems, and **stress** and help them identify a trusted adult they can talk to if they are struggling. Let them know they are not alone.

It can feel scary to talk about Suicide, but in my experience, it is important to talk directly with adolescents to help them deal with this topic. If you are unsure how to talk with your teen about Suicide, **connect them with a therapist** or guidance counsellor who can help them process any feelings they might be having. Know you are not alone, either. Together, hopefully, lives can be saved.

© Copyright 2018 GoodTherapy.org. All rights reserved. Permission to publish granted by **Katelyn Alcamo, LCMFT, therapist in Bethesda, Maryland**

Raising Awareness on World Suicide Prevention Day
September 10, 2015

Contributed by Zawn Villines

September 10 is World Suicide Prevention Day, and organizations worldwide are raising awareness about **Suicide and suicide prevention**. In 2010, the Centres for Disease Control and Prevention reported 38,364 suicides for that year—an average of 105 each day. In 2013, Suicide was responsible for 41,149 deaths. A million adults (0.5% of the population) attempt suicide each year, and 2.2 million (1% of the population) say they made a suicide plan in the last year.

On Twitter, users are discussing the issue using the hashtag **#worldsuicidepreventionday**.

RAISING AWARENESS: FACTS ABOUT SUICIDE

Suicidal thoughts are common among people facing issues such as **depression** and **anxiety**. Some key statistics to know on World Suicide Prevention Day include:

- Suicide is the tenth leading cause of death for all ages and the third leading cause of death for youth ages 10-24.
- Many people survive suicide attempts, but these attempts can produce **lifelong injuries**. A survey of high school students found that 8% tried to kill themselves in the last year. For every 25 suicide attempts, one is successful.
- Men represent 79% of all suicides and are four times more likely to kill themselves than women.
- One person in the world dies by Suicide every 40 seconds.

- Access to firearms dramatically increases the Risk of Suicide. Firearms, suffocation, and poisoning are the top three methods of youth suicide.

WARNING SIGNS OF SUICIDE

People who kill themselves may make threats to do so, but suicidal people do not always act depressed. Some may even seem better after they develop a suicide plan. Depression and other **mental health issues** and a **recent loss** can be significant predictors of Suicide. Some other warning signs include:

- Talking about killing oneself, feeling trapped, or **feeling hopeless**—the more detailed and concrete the suicide plan, the higher the risk of Suicide is.
- Reckless behaviour, such as abusing drugs or alcohol, taking more risks, or disregarding the feelings and safety of others
- Giving things away or making a plan for after death
- Increased **aggression**
- Calling or visiting loved ones to say goodbye
- Unpleasant and overwhelming emotions, such as hostility, **sadness**, anxiety, or **irritability**

HELPING A LOVED ONE

If someone you know threatens Suicide or displays warning signs that he or she might commit Suicide, take them seriously. People do not typically threaten Suicide for attention. Instead, try the following steps:

- Listen to your loved one, and offer **compassion** and **empathy** without judgment. Minimizing his or her feelings, shaming him or her for suicidal impulses, or telling your loved one, you will not listen to him or her can increase painful **emotions**, thereby increasing the risk of Suicide.

- Do not keep your loved one's feelings a secret. Seek help to keep him or her safe. Tell a parent, teacher, spouse, or other loved one who may be able to help, particularly if the person is a child. Choose whom to tell selectively; if a teenager is upset about an abusive parent, for instance, it might be better to tell a teacher or grandparent.

- Remove means of committing Suicide, such as weapons and pills.

- Stay with the person if you are concerned Suicide is imminent.

- Ask your loved one to agree to delay the Suicide for a day, a week, or a month to see if things get better.

- Offer a distraction. Sometimes the pain of depression or a loss coupled with isolation or boredom can worsen suicidal feelings. Offer to take your loved one to lunch or to an activity he or she has previously enjoyed.

- Encourage your loved one to seek help, and reassure him or her that **therapy can work**.

If you need help immediately, contact the **Help-lines mentioned.** You can call any time to seek help for yourself or a loved one. Remember that the hotline is a crisis intervention tool—not a substitute for therapy or loving support from friends and family.

References:

1. National Suicide Prevention Lifeline. (n.d.). Retrieved from http://www.suicidepreventionlifeline.org/gethelp/someone.aspx
2. Preventing Suicide: Reaching out and saving lives. (n.d.). Retrieved from https://www.iasp.info/wspd/
3. *Suicide facts at a glance* [PDF]. (n.d.). Atlanta: Centers for Disease Control and Prevention.
4. Suicide facts. (n.d.). Retrieved from http://www.save.org/index.cfm?fuseaction=home.viewPage&page_id=705D5DF4-055B-F1EC-3F66462866FCB4E6
5. Suicide prevention. (2015, March 10). Retrieved from http://www.cdc.gov/violenceprevention/pub/youth_suicide.html

When Life Continues:
Recovering from a Suicide Attempt
February 15, 2019

by Crystal Raypole

If you or a loved one is **in crisis**, *you can call*

The Help-lines mentioned above

Surviving a **suicide** attempt can lead to a range of intense emotions and feelings. Many people report feeling a new sense of hope or believing they survived for a reason. Others might feel renewed hopelessness or begin to have thoughts of making another attempt. Some people think love and compassion from friends and family. Others might feel increasingly alone.

Other emotions might include:

- Relief, or being glad the attempt failed
- Disappointment or confusion
- Embarrassment and shame
- Fatigue, lethargy, or general overwhelm.
- Anger

Whatever feelings you experience, it's essential to **work with a counsellor** trained in helping people recover from suicide attempts. Healing from a suicide attempt is possible, though recovery time may vary depending on different factors. According to **Tamara Hill, MS, NCC, CCTP, LPC**, "Recovery is possible with planning, but recovery should be multi-dimensional."

GETTING HELP AFTER A SUICIDE ATTEMPT

One of the first steps in recovering from a suicide attempt is seeking health care. It's important to get medical attention for any physical injuries or illnesses related to the attempt. A mental health professional will talk to you at the hospital to see how you're feeling and whether you're still at risk for Suicide. If you're already working with a therapist, the hospital can contact them.

If you're still in crisis or your doctor or counsellor is concerned for your safety, they may recommend you remain in the hospital as a patient until your suicide risk has decreased. People at high risk for Suicide who don't want to be admitted to the hospital may be hospitalized involuntarily for a few days. This isn't common. It's only likely to happen if your care providers believe you are very likely to attempt Suicide again very soon. You may not want to stay in the hospital, but remaining somewhere safe is a good idea if you plan to make another attempt.

It's important that you prioritize your healing and spend time with people who can offer support. Some of your loved ones may need time to work through their own feelings, but you can only be responsible for your own recovery. Once you're home, your friends and family may ask questions you aren't sure how to answer. Suicide is a topic that's still surrounded by **stigma**, so it can be difficult to talk about what you experienced.

Remember that you don't have to share anything you don't want to. If you're going to talk to your loved ones but need more time, let them know you're still sorting through your feelings. Your counsellor can help you work through what to say if you're struggling to find the right words.

You've just experienced something very traumatic. Your family and friends may be affected by your decision to attempt Suicide. Some people may say thoughtless or hurtful things out of grief or fear. It's important that you prioritize your healing and spend time with people who can offer support. Some of your loved ones may need time to work through their own feelings, but you can only be responsible for your own recovery.

HOW LONG DOES IT TAKE TO RECOVER FROM A SUICIDE ATTEMPT?

Recovery from attempted Suicide can take time. The amount of time may depend on several factors, including the level of social/emotional support you have and how you continue to work through the challenges affecting your mental health.

Recovery typically happens in stages. A study published in the *Journal of Clinical Nursing* lists five common phases of recovery:

- People realize that they still have a business in life and don't want to die.
- A person becomes aware that they need to seek help from others, such as professionals or loved ones.
- A person re-encounters **stress** and hardship in their life.
- A person adjusts their behaviour to cope better with life's challenges.
- A person accepts that there are good and bad parts to life and begins to invest in their own well-being.

The same study suggests the recovery is often nonlinear. People often move back and forth between stages of self-awareness, adjustment, and acceptance. A person may feel average one day, stressed the next, and then hopeful the third.

Self-care is an important part of recovery.

- You can physically take care of yourself by getting enough sleep, taking any medications your doctor or **psychiatrist** prescribed, making time for physical activity, and eating nourishing foods.
- Activities such as listening to music, writing in a journal, or working with your hands or body can help you feel better emotionally.
- Many people find yoga and meditation to be both emotionally and physically beneficial.

These things can all have a positive impact on recovery.

THERAPY FOR SUICIDE RECOVERY

In many cases, the triggers leading to a suicide attempt don't go away after the attempt. If you were working with a therapist before attempting Suicide but therapy wasn't helping, consider trying a new approach to treatment. Not every approach works for every person. Talk with your therapist about what's working and what isn't. If there's a new concern in your life that's adding stress, try to address this in therapy so you can develop ways to cope.

Check-in frequently with your therapist, and be honest about what you're feeling. Your therapist's job is to help you, and they are trained to do so with compassion and without judgment. Another important component of therapy after a suicide attempt is developing your crisis/safety plan. According to Hill, this plan might include "triggers, warning signs of evident regression in health, and a concrete plan of **coping skills** to use to avoid hospitalization or suicide attempts." Hill goes on to emphasize the importance of societal support, which might include "addresses to local groups, registration information to educational seminars, and websites to local organizations that support suicide recovery."

Your therapist can help you develop a safety plan. Check in frequently with your therapist, and be honest about what you're feeling. Your therapist's job is to help you, and they are trained to do so with compassion and without judgment.

If you have family support (or support from your partner or close friends), consider including them in your recovery plan and therapy if possible. Suicide is a difficult topic, and your family and friends may not know how to talk to you about what happened. They may be working through their own feelings about the attempt. Therapy can provide a safe space for you and your loved ones to share your thoughts—when you're ready to do so.

PREVENTING FUTURE SUICIDE ATTEMPTS

Making one suicide attempt is a risk factor for future suicide attempts. A 2014 review of articles looking at Suicide found that one in 25 people who are hospitalized for **self-harm** complete suicide within five years. A 2016 study looking at 1,490 people who attempted Suicide found almost 82% of those who didn't complete their first attempt completed a second attempt within one year.

It's important to have a crisis plan when recovering from a suicide attempt. This is something you might talk about with your therapist. Your crisis plan might include:

- A list of what triggers suicidal thoughts or feelings.
- A list of things that help you cope with triggers.
- A list (or photos) of your loved ones, pets, and other things that are important to you. These can help you cope in a time of crisis.
- Names and numbers of people you can reach out to, such as friends, family, your therapist, and doctor, or others you trust.

- Numbers for immediate care, such as the nearest emergency room, a suicide helpline, or other emergency services.
- A list of steps to keep yourself safe if you are in crisis. For example, you might plan how you could avoid or get rid of items in your house that you could harm yourself with.

It's also important to seek support from others. Re-establishing connections with people who care for you can have a significant impact on recovery. Different people in your life can help in different ways, so don't be afraid to reach out to the people who care about you.

It helps to be clear about what you need. For example, if you don't feel like talking, you could ask family members or close friends if they can keep you company when you're struggling to cope with difficult feelings. You might say something like, "I don't want to talk, but I want to distract myself from thinking about hurting myself. Can we go for a walk?"

After surviving a suicide attempt, you may feel lost and uncertain of your next steps. The journey forward may seem long and difficult. But recovery is possible! Take the time you need to heal and make sure you have social and professional support as you work toward recovery. Remember, you are not alone. There is **hope** for the future.

References:

1. After an attempt. (n.d.). American Foundation for Suicide Prevention. Retrieved from https://afsp.org/find-support/ive-made-attempt/after-an-attempt

2. Bostwick, J. M., Pabbati, C., Geske, J. R., & McKean, A. J. (2016, August 13). Suicide attempt as a risk factor for completed Suicide: Even more lethal than we knew. *The American Journal of Psychiatry, 173*(11), 1094-1100. Retrieved from https://ajp.psychiatryonline.org/doi/full/10.1176/appi.ajp.2016.15070854

3. Carrigan, C. G., & Lynch, D. J. (2003). Managing suicide attempts: Guidelines for the primary care physician. *The Primary Care Companion to the Journal of Clinical Psychiatry, 5*(4) 169-174. Retrieved from https://www.ncbi.nlm.nih.gov/pmc/articles/PMC419387

4. Carroll, R., Metcalfe, C., & Gunnell, D. (2014, February 28). Hospital presenting self-harm and risk of fatal and non-fatal repetition: Systematic review and meta-analysis. *PLoS ONE, 9*(2). Retrieved from https://journals.plos.org/plosone/article?id=10.1371%2Fjournal.pone.0089944

5. Chi, M. T., Long, A., Jeang, S. R., Ku, Y. C., Lu, T., & Sun, F. K. (2014). Healing and recovering after a suicide attempt: A grounded theory study. *Journal of Clinical Nursing, 23*(11-12), 1751-1759. Retrieved from https://www.ncbi.nlm.nh.gov/pubmed/24251862

6. Recovering after a suicide attempt. (n.d.). SuicideLine Victoria. Retrieved from https://www.suicideline.org.au/resource/recovering-after-a-suicide-attempt

7. Sellin, L., Asp, M., Kumlin, T., Wallsen, T., & Gustin, L. W.

(2017, February 28). To be present, share and nurture: A lifeworld phenomenological study of relatives' participation in the suicidal person's recovery. *International Journal of Qualitative Studies in Health and Well-being, 12*(1). Retrieved from https://www.ncbi.nlm.nih.gov/pmc/articles/PMC5345596

8. *A journey toward health and hope* [PDF]. (2015). Substance Abuse and Mental Health Services Administration. Retrieved from https://store.samhsa.gov/system/files/sma15-4419.pdf

Help for suicidal thoughts - NHS

https://www.nhs.uk/conditions/Suicide

Information: Papyrus – for people under 35 Call 0800 068 41 41 – Monday to Friday 9am to 10pm, weekends and bank holidays 2pm to 10pm Text 07860 039967 Email pat@papyrus-uk.org

Suicide | Mental Health Foundation

https://www.mentalhealth.org.uk/a-to-z/s/suicide

Suicide behaviours are complex, there is no single explanation of why people die by **Suicide**. Social, psychological, and cultural factors can all interact to lead a person to suicidal thoughts or behaviour. For many people, an attempt may occur after a long period of suicidal thoughts or feelings, while in other cases, it may be more impulsive.

Myths about suicide | Samaritans

https://www.samaritans.org/./myths-about-suicide

- Myth: People who talk about Suicide aren't serious and won't go through with it. Fact: People who...
- Myth: If a person is serious about killing themselves then there's nothing you can do. Fact: Often...
- Myth: You have to be mentally ill to think about Suicide. Fact: 1 in 5 people have thought about...
- Myth: People who are suicidal want to die. Fact: The majority of people who feel suicidal do not...

If you feel you are in immediate danger to yourself or others, you can (dial 999 in UK) or go to the nearest emergency hospital room.

Ways to Cope with Grief and Loss of a Pet

In the United States, there are almost as many pets as there are adult humans. Collectively, Americans keep 60 million dogs, 70 million cats, and a host of other animals as pets. More than half of all <u>families</u> in the U.S. have at least one pet, and many of those families consider their pets to be members of the family. Although the actual science is hard to quantify, most pet owners believe that their animal companion enriches the quality of their lives, which is why it can be so painful when they die.

Losing a beloved animal companion can be a heart-rending experience. Having to make the decision to euthanize a long- and still-cherished pet is arguably even more difficult. People often struggle with overwhelming feelings of grief, loss, and guilt after choosing to put their pets to sleep. These strong feelings that accompany euthanizing a pet come as the result of their roles in our lives and the strong bonds we are capable of developing with animals. In fact, research by Jaroleman indicates that the bond between people and their pets can have a direct impact on physical and mental health.

While losing a pet can affect us in profound ways and may be quite painful, there are several strategies that might be employed to help people cope successfully after putting a pet to sleep.

PREPARE FOR THE GRIEVING PROCESS

Our animal companions provide us with love, support, and loyalty, and they often fulfill an important psychological need. When we are faced with the decision to euthanize our pets, it is the end of an important relationship—for some, one of the most important relationships in their lives. Many pet owners will experience some form of the grief, though each person will grieve differently.

Do not be surprised if the pain you feel after putting your pet to sleep is deeper and sharper than you initially anticipated, so take the time you need to complete the grieving process. Losing companionship is never easy and it may take some time for you to come to terms with the changes in your family and life.

SEEK OUT SOCIAL SUPPORT

When we lose a close relative in death, the world around us tends to help us move through the grieving process. Family and friends may draw closer together for some time, we take time off from work, and people generally offer their support. The loss of a pet, however, is often met with much less sympathy or support. For example, a survey conducted by Quackenbush and Glickman revealed that 45% of pet owners that had lost a pet missed one to three days of work, even though most employers do not consider the loss of a pet to be grounds for bereavement leave.

While our immediate family members and veterinarians are likely able to relate to the pain we feel and offer needed support, some expect us to just "get on with it." The world around us simply does not understand that our pet was not "just a dog" and that we cannot "just get a new one."

According to research by Clements, Benasutti, and Carmone, "The loss or death of a pet, and the surrounding traumatic events, can unbalance existing social roles and family relationships, and can result in the disruption of dyadic relationships between the owner and other significant people (spouse, children, and colleagues)."

It is important not to push our friends and family members away, especially during this stressful time, and it may be helpful to open up to them and share our feelings. After all, who better to remind us of the wonderful times we shared together with our now departed pets?

If you don't feel comfortable talking about how much your pet meant to you with your family and friends, consider making an appointment with a therapist. A therapist can provide healing support and help you understand the grieving process better. With time, he or she can provide tools and coping strategies to help you return to a normal life without your pet.

ANTICIPATE A CHANGE IN ROUTINE AND STAY BUSY WITH MEANINGFUL ACTIVITIES

Pet owners develop habits around their pets due to the dependency pets have on their human companions. Their very lives are at stake. Dedicated pet owners often set aside times for feeding, washing, and walking or exercising pets. For some people, their pets might even serve as living, breathing alarm clocks.

Humans are creatures of habit. We like to know what to expect and are comforted by the fact we exert a measure of control over our actions and responsibilities, but losing a pet dramatically alters that sense of routine and predictability. Quackenbush and Glickman's survey of pet owners that had recently lost a pet found that 93% reported a disruption of their daily routines and 70% of respondents said their social activities diminished.

Considering this, it is easy to understand the <u>emptiness</u> a person might feel as he or she learns how to deal with life after a pet has been euthanized. Each day is now filled with standardized voids and blocks of time with nothing to do and no animal companion to fill them.

To help soothe your grief, fill these time slots with fun and meaningful activities, especially in the company of supportive companions. Play board games, go to the park, or have a dinner party—anything you might enjoy. You might even consider making a donation to an animal-rights charity in the name of your recently deceased pet. Here are a few other suggestions for activities that may help you heal:

- Volunteer your time to a local animal shelter.

- To memorialize your pet, consider making a donation of needed items to a local animal shelter. You can ask family and friends to donate, which might present a good opportunity to talk about your deceased pet with them.

- Learn about therapeutic approaches to coping with grief, loss, and bereavement. Consider reaching out to a therapist to learn more.

- If you are experiencing guilt about euthanizing your pet, write a truthful letter addressed to your deceased animal friend about all the reasons you chose to do it. This may help you work through your guilt by addressing the practical, and perhaps merciful, reasons for your decision.

References:

1. Clements, P. T., Benasutti, K. M., & Carmone, A. (2003). Support for bereaved owners of pets. *Perspectives in Psychiatric Care, 39*(2), 49-54. Retrieved from http://search.proquest.com/docview/200756802?accountid=1229

2. Jaroleman, J. (1998). A comparison of the reaction of children and adults: Focusing on pet loss and bereavement. *Omega, 37*, 133-150.

3. Quackenbush, J. E., & Glickman, L. (1984). Helping people adjust to the death of a pet. *Health and Social Work 9*(1), 42-48.

4. Sable, P. (1995). Pets, attachment, and well-being across the life cycle. *Social Work, 40*(3), 334-41. Retrieved from http://search.proquest.com/docview/215272292?accountid=1229

5. Spencer, S., Decuypere, E., Aerts, S., & De Tavernier, J. (2006). History and ethics of keeping pets: Comparison with farm animals. *Journal of Agricultural and Environmental Ethics, 19*(1), 17-25. doi:http://dx.doi.org/10.1007/s10806-005-4379-

Coping with Cancer

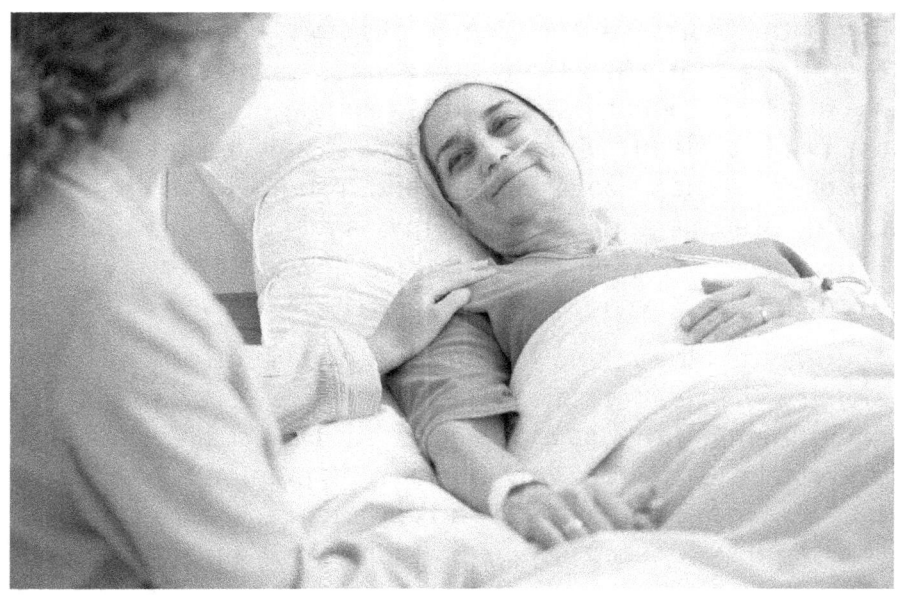

How Diagnosis Affected My Mental Health

Contributed by Maia Delmoor, MS, LPC, CAADC

In June 2017, I was diagnosed with metastatic sarcoma. I went from being a healthy, practicing therapist who worked three jobs while also caring for my two children and husband, to being afraid to move.

The impact of hearing the possibility of cancer was crippling, even at first. But once it was confirmed, in a matter of days my body began to fall apart as I lost the mental capacity to will myself to keep moving.

See, before I even knew something was wrong, I had already begun to *feel* that something was wrong. I was extremely fatigued, and each day my movements became slower. I became more irritated and unable to engage in regular activity with my children and husband. They all thought it was due to the hours I worked, as did I. But the reality was that my body was rapidly shutting down on me. Then, when I heard the word "cancer," I mentally and emotionally broke! Everything that I had been doing was for the betterment of my family, but what was the cost? I could not believe I was on the brink of death without having first enjoyed my life. With my eyes on the prize, the so-called finish line, I had lost sight of the present and neglected my family. Now I wondered, "How do I get myself through this? How do I get my family through this? How do I prepare them for what is to come?"

The mental fatigue and the loss of bodily control that comes along with a cancer diagnosis can cause great stress. The components of the diagnosis and treatment regime can easily overwhelm a person. Any number of mental health issues may develop along with such an experience. Feeling emotions like sadness, uncertainty, even guilt is not uncommon, and these may become difficult to control. In some cases, denial and dissociation might also be present.

Challenging and difficult feelings can flood in at any time, unexpectedly, especially when in the "eye of the storm," so to speak. Often, once an appropriate treatment regime is identified and begun, emotional displays may become less frequent. You might begin to feel more stable, even with the side effects that occur as a result of treatment. Fear of the unknown may begin to dissipate, and you may become calmer and surer of what is going on.

A CANCER DIAGNOSIS' EMOTIONAL TOLL

Looking back and reflecting on my patterns of thought and behaviors, I believe I was experiencing what is classified in the Diagnostic and Statistical Manual of Mental Disorders *(DSM-5)* as an adjustment disorder with mixed anxiety and depressed mood. The *DSM-5* specifies that symptoms of an adjustment disorder appear within three months of a stressful event (such as divorce, accident, loss, serious medical diagnosis, or any major life change). The symptoms usually dissipate after the effects of the stressors subside, unless the effects are chronic. More specifically, an adjustment disorder can be compounded with symptoms of depression and/or anxiety. In short, this diagnosis is typically characterized by a combination of alternating depressed and anxious mood symptoms that create difficulties for self/others with regard to daily function.

Although I did not meet the full criteria for a diagnosis of major depression or anxiety, I definitely felt symptoms related to both. Not only was I depressed due to the severity of my illness, I was anxious every time I had to go to the doctor, worrying about things like being late for my appointment. I had several incidents when having my port accessed, so I began to feel like there was going to be a problem each time, and whenever it was accessed I went into a state of panic. All I could do was imagine the pain and worry that something was going to go wrong and/or that my body would not respond to the medicine correctly. I even experienced a range of emotions when I thought of other people seeing me. I was afraid that others wouldn't accept me, that I was I ugly without hair. My daughter cried and could barely look at me after I had to shave my head. I was devastated by her reaction and depressed at the thought of her not wanting to be around me when I looked the way I did, and I interchangeably felt both depressed and anxious.

Although my stressor was indeed traumatic, I did not experience avoidance or dissociation, necessary criteria for a diagnosis of acute stress disorder or posttraumatic stress. I knew had to attack the cancer like it was attacking me: aggressively. I had to attend doctor visits and be compliant with directives, no matter how scared or angry I became.

COPING AND ACCEPTANCE

In accepting my diagnosis of cancer, many things ran through my head. My hopelessness was real, as was the lack of desire—and lack of ability—to engage in my usual activities. I quickly became overwhelmed by nervousness at the thought of surgeries, treatments, and the perceptions surrounding my changed appearance. While trying to make sense of the changes that have occurred, I found that maladaptive thought patterns were trying to take root. Even beliefs I recognized as irrational began to filter through with all the information I was trying to process.

Therapy is a positive and important step we can take to help counteract the emotional and mental effects of a cancer diagnosis.

I cycled through questions: "How do I fight this?" "Can I survive this?" "Why *me*?" "How will my family be affected?" If I can't work, how will I pay my bills?" "What will I do next, once I beat this?"

These and many other questions loomed over me, and I didn't have the answers to any of them. I knew I had to identity some coping strategies fast. Luckily for me, my support network assembled quickly.

A support network is everything! Without one, the emotional upheaval of a cancer diagnosis (or any other major illness) can be catastrophic. A support network is formed from a number of different individuals, including but not limited to:

- Family, immediate and extended
- Friends
- A support group
- Religious leader and church community

- The organizations that exist to support people diagnosed with cancer by helping out with meals, beautification rituals, and babysitting or cleaning services.

Along with the physical support of health care and modern medicine, we also need emotional support. Having a good laugh, engaging in prayer or meditation, or even just sitting with a trusted person so we know we aren't alone, is paramount. It can often help relieve some of the depression and anxiety that comes with the reality of a cancer diagnosis. While it's important to allow ourselves to fully experience and sit with our emotions, a good support system helps to keep us grounded, which in turn helps minimize the development of maladaptive though patterns as we begin to cope with the reality of living with cancer.

Seeking support from a trained mental health professional, such as a therapist or counse lor, can also be helpful. Therapy is a positive and important step we can take to help counteract the emotional and mental effects of a cancer diagnosis. Keep in mind that many people in our support networks are trying to cope with their own emotions surrounding our state of being. Sometimes, it may be hard for them to truly hear what we are feeling and engage with us. When your support system is unable or unequipped to handle our emotional state, a (trained) source of non-judgmental, outside support is beneficial. Therapy offers a safe space where we can be unapologetic and candid with what we are feeling and why.

As I moved forward, I realized the importance of creating and engaging in hobbies. When we are sick, we may have a lot of idle time. When idle, many of us tend to overthink a particular situation or fixate on distressing thoughts. In my case, I found that keeping myself busy, as much as I was able, helped keep thoughts of self-doubt and self-pity from settling in.

Currently, I am actively engaging in chemotherapy, and I still struggle with my cancer diagnosis. Holding on to past patterns of normalcy may be difficult or even impossible for some. I've found it's actually easier to identify the positives of my situation.

By altering my expectations of self to reflect my present state of being, I have made hope easier to obtain. I believe life is not supposed to be the same experience it was five years ago. Every day we evolve, gaining and losing certain aspects of life as time goes by. I may have lost a job, a friend, or some health freedoms, but I have gained wisdom; love; and a greater appreciation of self, life, and family. It is all right to be different from your past self, and it's all right to be comfortable in your new self. It's also normal to feel sadness, fear, and anger as part of the grieving process of shedding the old.

This is a new chapter of my life, one that is not without great difficulty. But I've learned to lean on my support system (my village) to take the steps necessary to embrace what lies before me.

Maia Delmoor, a licensed counsellor and GoodTherapy.org member who specializes in the treatment of trauma and addictions, was diagnosed with cancer in 2017.

Care for the Caregiver: After the Loss

Contributed by Ivan Chan, MA, MFT

A common experience for caregivers after a loss is a feeling of purposelessness.

After having one's schedule tightly wrapped around the needs of an ailing partner, parent, child, friend, or patient, their death can leave one not only heartbroken but also searching for how to fill the days once again.

The background worry does not need to be there anymore. The routine of administering medications has vanished. The limitations of travel, vacation, and socializing with others have been lifted. Grocery shopping is a reminder of what favourite foods not to bring home. And one's thoughts, feelings, and actions are directed at the wide and lonely expanse of an unexpected future, with no apparent road map or even the motivation to move forward.

Adding to the sense of emptiness, outside supports oftentimes disappear, too. If one was caring for someone terminally ill, the presence of hospice might have been part of the schedule, providing comfort and companionship; however, after the death, hospice leaves and the caregiver remains. Likewise, family, friends, and neighbours who had been visiting regularly may suddenly or slowly evaporate after a time, or also after the death, making the home seem more silent than it ever was in the past.

It is hard to imagine what it will be like without the mission of caring for someone. It is nearly impossible to conceive of what it will be like to live without making sure that someone is still there and still comfortable.

Amidst the rioting emotions of grief or the numbing shock of coming to the edge of the world and peering into nothing is the invitation to look back. Dwelling on the past keeps one stuck in the past, but searching the past for a forgotten experience or lesson can unlock our present and future.

Questions and thoughts to consider, in no particular order:
- What did I do with my time before I provided care?
- I was not always a caregiver; I was also (fill in the blank with past roles, jobs, etc.)
- I've always dreamed of (fill in the blank with an activity, destination, goal, etc.)
- What were my hobbies before I became a caregiver?
- What and who have I ignored while providing care that I can attend to now?

Most of us thrive on having some sort of structure in our lives, whether that is from being caregivers or from the jobs that we do or the roles that we play in our families and communities. The structures can be dictated by us, or given to us by affection, obligation, or authority.

After a death, it is natural to feel as if what held our lives together has fallen apart, as if the universe suddenly stopped making sense and the unspoken meaning that glued our lives together has ceased to hold us together. Why wait in the grocery line? What's the point of getting out of bed? Why does anything matter, when what mattered to us has been taken away? All structure seems to be rubble at our feet.

It is important for those who feel a lack of purpose to acknowledge this loss of structure. It does not matter what someone else feels or thinks about their grief or yours, or if they seem to pick up and resume a "normal" life. We are each laid low by different blows we receive in life, and comparison is rarely useful in mourning. We pick ourselves up as we can, and as we need to.

Recreating structure can be challenging, but it can be accomplished. Returning to old structures we had left behind can offer us guidance in the days to come, if not a welcome distraction to the new and unknown path ahead. If one looks to the past for memories, experiences, and what provided a sense of purpose before providing care, this search can help create a new structure, new routine, or "new normal" to live by.

When Loss Hurts: 6 Physical Effects of Grief

by GoodTherapy Staff

If you have ever lost a loved one, you have most likely experienced grief. Grief is an intense feeling of sadness or sorrow. It is generally brought on by the loss of something or someone. The end of a long-term relationship, like a divorce, or the death of a family member may cause grief.

Grief is not always thought of as a full-body experience. But just as grief can affect mental health, it can also have physical aspects. Physical symptoms may not come with every kind of grief. But intense grief—for example, that caused by the death of a child or partner—can bring about side effects that may feel more physical than anything else.

Grief can trigger a number of mental health symptoms and issues. These might include depression, loneliness, and anxiety. The line between the grief period and a mental health issue may be hard to define. It can help to consult a trusted therapist or counsellor if you are having trouble with grief or similar feelings.

Knowing which symptoms of grief to watch for may allow you to soothe and address any affects you experience.

1. HEART PROBLEMS

Heart problems can be brought on by intense stress in a variety of situations. But there are particular heart risks associated with grief. One study found the death of a loved one to increase a person's chance of a heart attack.

There's also a specific temporary syndrome brought on by the death of a loved one called *takotsubo cardiomyopathy*, or "broken heart syndrome." Broken heart syndrome is caused by a disruption in the blood being pumped to one section of the heart. Because of this, it mimics the effects of a heart attack—chest pain and shortness of breath—but is temporary. People with broken heart syndrome can undergo treatment for it. They may also choose to wait for the syndrome to reverse itself in a few weeks.

It is important to note that if you experience chest pain or shortness of breath over a long period of time, you should consult your doctor for deeper causes. This is true for any other severe or long-lasting physical effects of grief.

2. LOWERED IMMUNITY

Some people catch colds or come down with the flu during times of immense stress. They may notice they are more susceptible to these same ailments during a period of intense grieving. This is because in adults, grief can lower the immune system.

A 2014 study found that older adults experiencing grief, specifically due to the loss of a spouse, could not maintain a stress hormone balance. As a result, they experienced reduced neutrophil function. This means that during the grieving process, older adults are less likely to produce some types of white blood cells, leaving them prone to infections.

3. BODY ACHES AND PAINS

Aches and pains are a common physical symptom of grief. Grief can cause back pain, joint pain, headaches, and stiffness. The pain is caused by the overwhelming amount of stress hormones being released during the grieving process. These effectively stun the muscles they contact. Stress hormones act on the body in a similar way to broken heart syndrome. Aches and pains from grief should be temporary. If they persist over the long term, consult your physician.

4. DIGESTIVE ISSUES

The digestive tract can be sensitive to times of intense stress. It can be all too common to seek comfort in food during stressful periods or to experience a queasy stomach when anxious. Grief inspires these symptoms and others, such as a loss of appetite, binge eating, nausea, and irritable bowel syndrome.

Knowing these symptoms are caused by grief can help alleviate them. When you feel an urge to eat when sad or notice you haven't eaten all day because of that same sadness, it can be a good indicator to call a trusted friend or licensed mental health professional to set up an appointment.

5. UNHEALTHY COPING MECHANISMS

Overeating or not eating enough during the grieving process is only one unhealthy coping mechanism people may experience. Some can be more harmful than others. People may turn to alcohol or cigarettes, the overuse of which can have long-lasting effects on the liver and lungs.

Others may engage in self-harming behavior, drug use, or other high-risk behaviors. All of these coping mechanisms can have intensely damaging, long-lasting effects on the body and brain. If you find yourself frequently engaging in behaviors like these to cope with grief, it is crucial you reach out to a trusted friend or licensed professional for help.

6. SLEEP PROBLEMS AND FATIGUE

A 2017 study found that spouses who were bereaved by suicide had a higher risk of developing sleep issues. Sleep is supposed to be when the body and brain rest and repair themselves. Sleep disruption during grief can be especially frustrating. It can be debilitating to constantly feel both sad, anxious, and exhausted. Insomnia can be a common occurrence in those who are grieving. But it should only be temporary. A continued inability to sleep regularly or feel rested should be reported to your doctor.

WHEN GRIEF BECOMES A CYCLE

Many people aspire to finish grieving and move on with their lives in a healthy way. But some may find this is harder than expected. It is possible for grief to become a cycle. Sometimes memories of loss or of a lost loved one may light up the reward receptors in the brain. This means that moving on or "letting go" can be much more difficult. Those memories and the grieving process can feed into an addictive feeling.

A cycle of grief can take a toll on a person's physical and mental health. Continuing the grieving process for a long period of time means a person's risk for long-term health problems is increased. What could have been a short-term symptom—chest pain, stomach aches, or sleep problems, for example—can manifest in much more serious ways. These could include heart disease, eating disorders, or chronic fatigue.

MANAGING GRIEF

It is important to seek help if you need it to regulate your mind-body connection. What gets thrown out of whack during the grieving process can, in fact, get back on track.

Building a healthy routine can be a first step to mitigating some of the physical symptoms of grief. Regular exercise and a nutritious diet can help with pain, heart risks, digestive issues, and sleep patterns. Talking about grief with family and friends or a licensed mental health professional can help address the grief directly. Doing so may also foster the development of healthy coping skills.

It is important to remember you are not alone. Asking for help may an important step during the grieving process. It can take time to heal, and that is normal. Grief cannot be rushed. But with love and compassion from family, and the help of a therapist, grief can come to an end.

References:

1. Addicted to grief? Chronic grief activates pleasure areas of the brain. (2008, June 22). Retrieved from https://www.sciencedaily.com/releases/2008/06/080620195446.htm

2. Broken heart syndrome. (2016, November 5). Retrieved from https://www.mayoclinic.org/diseases-conditions/broken-heart-syndrome/symptoms-causes/syc-20354617

3. Erlangsen, A., et al. (2017). Association between spousal suicide and mental, physical, and social health outcomes. *JAMA Psychiatry, 74*(5), 456-464. doi: 10.1001/jamapsychiatry.2017.0226

4. Gahles, N. (2016, November 22). The physical trauma of grief and loss. Retrieved from

https://www.integrativepractitioner.com/topics/news/body-trauma-grief

5. Mostofsky, E., Maclure, M., Sherwood, J. B., Tofler, G. H., Muller, J. E., & Mittleman, M. A. (2012, January 23). Risk of acute myocardial infarction after death of a significant person in one's life. *Circulation, 3*(125), 491-496. doi: 10.1161/CIRCULATIONAHA.111.061770

6. Qin, H., Cheng, C., Tang, X., Bian, Z. (2014, October 21). Impact of psychological stress on irritable bowel syndrome. *World Journal of Gastroenterology, 20*(39), 126-131. doi: 10.3748/wjg.v20.i39.14126

7. Vitlic, A., Khanfer, R., Lord, J. M., Carroll, D., Philips, A. C. (2014, August 29). Bereavement reduces neutrophil oxidative burst only in older adults: role of the HPA axis and immune senescence. *Immunity & Ageing, 11*(13). doi: 10.1186/1742-4933-11-13

What Happens After Death

I have had an opportunity working in a hospice over twenty years as a Volunteer. I have been very fortunate to perform various roles over this period. I worked on the reception desk, served on the Snack Bar and Shop, attended the patients and their family and friends, helped fund raising team, learned and achieved many skills, attended many studies, represented Hospice as an Ambassador. A few years I had gained education to facilitate the counseling department and provide support to many scholars in their research about psychology, psychotherapy.

Each role had provided me a different experience about the end of life. I gazed through people's emotions, behaviours, apprehensions, fears, anxiety, loss, grieving, praying and mourning. Hospice is a great place to learn about Life and Death.

Every day brings a new experience, new challenge and knowledge. To say that it has enriched my thoughts, would be an understatement. I have a different prospect of my life since I joined the Hospice. It has taught me, patience, empathy, value of family and friends, power of faith, our prayers and accepting God's will. Besides, It taught me how important it is to show your true emotions to your family and friends while you got a chance. It has taught me 'However good or bad situation is, it will pass.'

I feel privileged and humbled that people had trusted me with their feelings, experiences, emotions, and their past and present situations. I have felt their pain, their loss and their grief. Often, I cried with them. I have listened to their stories with compassion, provided them the space so that they could express themselves freely without being judged, encouraged them to adjust to their new Norm [Normal]. If I am unable to help, signposted them to others. People face unimaginable situations, sometime all they need is someone to listen to them. Most of them are so full up that they are just waiting for a chance to offload. That is why; it is said that 'listening is the hardest communication skill. Assuring someone that their secrets are safe with you is the hardest thing to do, but once you have gained their confidence, it is most valuable privilege that you become a friend for life. I have experienced on many occasions, when people stopped me and said 'you remember me, you helped me through a time when I need a shoulder to cry'. The satisfaction it gives, the fulfilment of a role is uncomprehensive. I look back and I often thank God providing me this opportunity.

The Sentiments included...

"They say there is a reason,
They say the time will heal.
But neither time nor reason
Will change the way I feel.

No one Knows the heartache behind the smiles
No one knows how many times, I've broken down & cries

I want to tell you something, there won't be any doubt
You are wonderful to think of, but so hard to be without.

Death leaves a heartache, no one can heal
You left memories, no one can steal

✯✯✯

"I thought of you with love to-day, but that is nothing new
I thought of you yesterday, and days before that too.
I think of you in silence, I often speak your name
All I have are memories, and your picture in frame.
Your memory is keepsake, with which I'll never part
God has you in His keeping, I have you in my heart.

Tony Bhaur

This poem was written by a teenager with a cancer, not long to live in New York Hospital

Slow Dance

Have you ever watched kids?

On a merry-go-round?

Or listened to the rain

Slapping on the ground?

Ever followed a butterfly's erratic flight?

Or Gazed at the sun into the fading night?

You better slow down.

Don't dance so fast.

Time is short.

The music won't last.

Do you run through each day?

On the fly?

When you ask How are you?

Do you hear a reply?

Life, Death and After

When the day is done
Do you lie in your bed?
With the next hundred chores
Running through your head?

You'd better slow down
Don't dance so fast.
Time is short.
The music won't last

Ever told your child,
We'll do it tomorrow?
And in your haste
Not see his sorrow?

Ever lost touch,
Let a good friendship die.
Cause you never had time
To call and say, 'Hi'

You'd better slow down.
Don't dance so fast.
Time is short.
The music won't last.

Tony Bhaur

When you run so fast to get somewhere
You miss half the fun getting there.
When you worry and hurry through your day,
It is like an unopened gift... thrown away.

Life is not a race.
Do take it slower
Hear the music
Before the song is over.

***

"Sorrow too deep for words."

"You never be more than thoughts away."

We look at three different aspects 'After Death' Practical, Emotional and Spiritual

Practical:

'Death' whether anticipated or not, we are never fully prepared. Even though we are in shock of a loss and the unknown fear without the deceased, we still have to do the necessaries. It has been said that very often the dispute erupts between the loved ones soon after the death. Everyone thinks that they know best and they are the special -one; everyone else should listen to them. It is not always the close family members often the others also get involved.

- Inform Family and friends

    People and relatives are scattered all over the world these days. There are different time zones. Special communication skills required, how to break the news. It is time consuming and emotionally draining. Very often some family members will object someone to participate

- Making arrangement for the release of the body

    If, the Death is by natural causes, Funeral directors often help for release of body from hospitals and home. They will store the body with dignity at their resting place. For other causes, it may require post-mortem. The corners or police may be involved. In some cases, there is a considerable delay obtaining the body.

    If the death had happened in the foreign land than the repatriation procedures have to be adhered to.

- Registering the death

    It depends where the death happened. If it is hospital, most of the hospitals have set procedures and they are very helpful. Death at home, accidental death, Victim of crime or disaster have different procedures. Obtaining a death certificate quickly is vital because you need to show it everywhere.

- Arranging funerals

    Whether it is burial or cremation. It still needs to be booked and paid for. Funerals are quite expensive these days. Often there are disputes regarding who is putting the bill? How it should be conducted? Who should be invited? What music? What food? What service? What faith? What Transport? Even, a dress code is becoming a problem these days. Flowers need to be arranged. Preparing the body and dressing the body need to be discussed.

- Tributes

    Usually, a discussion who is going to make tributes and in which order. There are only few heartfelt tributes. You could always tell which are those. Headstone, Benches, donations, memorials and legacies etc.

- Inform the authorities

    We need to inform the authorities, Banks, Building society, pensions, even the Taxman and so on. We still have to cancel the memberships, subscriptions, commitments, appointments, holidays and other bookings. Notify the utility providers. Close social media accounts. List is endless.

- Estate and Liabilities

    Sorting this, requires many skills. Reading the will, dealing with the wishes of the deceased, accepting the decisions. Dealing with the inheritance, probates and liabilities. Often, it is very difficult balance to draw between the memories and the expectations.

Emotional:

- Reflection on life:

    We have noticed that when someone is facing an imminent death. How often they want to make up with the people they had the disagreement or disputes or even animosity. They want to do things which they thought it is not in their nature to reconcile, because they felt they were right and others was wrong and it is not their part to make that first step. But when they are reflecting at this moment their egos, pride weakens and they don't want to leave it too late. It is not always one-way traffic. We also noticed once the people hear that someone, they had differences with, throughout their life, has a limited time they also want to make up and go to great lengths.

    One late evening, I was going by a patient's bed, he had no visitor and feeling lonely and sad. I pulled up my chair to talk to him. I do not know whether he was waiting for this moment or overwhelmed with his reflections. I was curious to know why people were not visiting him.

    I started, asking how was his day? Was he comfortable? Did he need anything? His answers were very brief and in very low tune. All of a sudden he said "I hope you are not in hurry' I could do with a talk". I noticed tears rolling down on his cheeks. I knew, this is the moment I have to make time and forget about any other commitments.

    I replied, 'My friend, I have all the time you need and I am all, yours'.

I drew the curtains around his bed and pulled my chair closer to his bed, took my jacket off and hung it behind the chair, put my phone away. I asked, 'shall I get you a drink or anything before we start'.

He answered, "No thanks". He composed himself, "I do appreciate this"

I leaned forward and looking attentively [listening pose]. 'I assure you that whatever, conversation we have, will be confidential and you can talk freely and without any hesitation or fear'

[This is the reason I am not going to mention the full conversation we had.] However, I will describe the main points of the conversation.

He was a managing director of leading company in our area. He started as a factory worker and progressed to establish a company of his own. His passion, hard work, devotion and drive made him, who he was at that time. But all the success in his business came at the cost of his relationship with his family and friends. Because he was too busy building his business that he had no time to socialise or attend to any social and family events.

He had a lovely wife, son and daughter. But his wife left him with his kids and set up a home away from him. Even though, he supported them financially very generously. He paid for his children's education and other needs but never had a relationship as a father. He blamed his wife for creating an atmosphere to turn his children against him. When the children completed their education, they migrated to take up their respective careers. Sadly, his wife died few years ago; he was not even invited to her funeral. He was bitter about it.

Then came a moment, when he posed and said; 'I want you

to help me to find a way for me to say good bye to my Children, and apologise for being such a horrible, selfish and arrogant Dad'.

I knew, he meant it and I was moved by his sincerity and willingness to reconcile. I had their contact details. I assured him that I would do my best to make that possible. I could see that he felt light as a big burden been taken away from his shoulders. I cannot remember, how many times he thanked me for listening to him and encouraging him to complete his message.

That night, I could not rest properly; I felt obliged and duty-bound. On the following morning; we started to make phone calls. His children were bitter too. Their first reaction was, they got nothing to do with his inheritance or anything else. But eventually, they agreed to attend his phone call, provided I was there to make sure he would not bring the past in and lecture them.

I am so glad to tell, the following day, we arranged the phone calls. First call was, with his daughter; both sides were hesitant, nervous and obviously with pauses and stops; then came openness, honesty and realisation of the circumstances. Eventually, tears and empathy. His son's conversation also adopted a similar pattern; but occasionally voice level went up and down. The pauses were longer as well.

We could all see; how calm he was after those calls. He was at peace. Sadly, his condition started to deteriorate, it became difficult for him to hold a conversation; two days later he passed away.

His daughter brought her own daughter to attend his funeral. She came to see me and brought a lovely thank you card which I treasure.

Closure:

There was another occasion; I was just signing in on the reception, I heard a mother sobbing loudly and speaking in Punjabi, [the language I can understand very well] in anguish, down the corridor. I turned around; she was astonished to see me there. She realised that I understood what she was saying and she felt bit embarrassed as well. I noticed that she was under enormous stress and she needed support, comfort and empathy.

I took her to a quiet- room. When she calmed down. I enquired what was the matter? She explained that 27-yrs-old her only son, whom she brought up on her own after her husband's death; was on his death bed. He had been living on his own. She added that he had been in a bad company lately. She then turned religious and always prayed for his well-being.

She even blamed herself, for not being educated and knowing the English Language to communicate fully with her son to guide him to right path and the career. She was still sobbing. She wanted to stay with her son, so that she can get a closure, she wanted to help him.

But he did not want her there and kept shouting "why won't you even let me die in peace; I know I have not been good but I do not want to be lectured anymore"

I brought her a cup of tea and went to see her son, on my own. He was very uncomfortable despite the pain management. I sat beside him and introduced myself. He was very pleased to see me. He was talking to me in Punjabi. We had a short conversation and I asked if I could be any help. Even before I could mention anything he said: "my mum is doing my head in and I want to rest" I explained him "She is upset and worried. You are the only child and she does not want to lose you. No parent wants their child to go before them. It is very difficult time. She does not know how to help and face the situation. Just imagine what she had gone through to raise you. She loves you so much but does not know how to express her feeling at the moment. In a way she had earned a right to be with you.

He interrupted me and said "But uncle, she keeps saying that I should do a path [recite the holy verses]; I don't know anything like that. I am a Lafanga [lay-about], I only went to gurdwara to have *parsad and langar* [food]. Tell me what good that will do to me now; isn't it too late?"

I said; 'you have called me an uncle that shows me that you are not bad at heart. I want you and your mum to have a peace. I want to make sure that you are comfortable while you are here and you get all the help you need. Your mum also deserves a closure. If you talk to each-other that will provide a comfort; If you don't mind, I also want to sit with you and learn about you' "Sure Uncle" he said calmly.

I fetched his mum to his bedside. We sat quietly for few moments and he asked "Just tell me; what does this path do?" I said: "let us all experience it". I went to his bathroom and prepared myself and brought his cap to cover his head.

I held his hand in my hand and started to do Sukhmani Sahib ji da Path [Sikh Prayer]. His mum also started to recite with me. Within a few minutes he closed his eyes, his breathing became calmer and calmer. We were experiencing unexplainable tranquillity and he started to squeeze my hand harder and harder. Sooner, the path finished he had a deep long breath and passed away. I always wondered what effect the path had on his soul!

- Last Wishes:

Over the years, we have experienced people making all sort of wishes, some strange, some odd and some laughable and unique. In the hospices most of the restrictions those are in ordinary hospitals get lifted. There is drink trolley going round twice a day. People who are smokers, they are even allowed to smoke in the designated areas. There is no limit on number of visitors. In some places, family members can stay overnight nearby or in the same room. There is complimentary therapy available for patients and their carers.

We have seen many marriages taking place. Some patients want to see and spend time with their pets. One lady who had stables wanted to spend her last day with her horse. So, the horse box was brought to the car park and her bed was wheeled to the car park so that she could spend some time with her beloved horse.

One farmer wanted to see the first lamb born on his farm that year. So, the three days old lamb was arranged to turn up at the hospice. Some wants to dress up as one of the special characters of a movie or play. We often have actors performing at the local theatre, come to the hospice and quite often they play a scene.

I even remember a lady who mentioned to me one evening that she spends every Wednesday night with her friends eating at this particular French restaurant. She was missing that; so, we rang the restaurant in questions and to our surprise a van pulled up and waiters came out and they served her favourite food with all the trimming.

Often, we get requests from the patients to meet their favourite players or manager from Local Football, Rugby, cricket or snooker. Some want to sing. Some wants to dance. Someone wants to sing or pray as a group.

- Hope:

Sometime against all the odds, things happen which nobody can explain. The similar event happened four years ago. A young mother of 32yrs old came to hospice. She overstayed on a student visa. She had two children taken into care because soon her partner found out that she got untreatable brain tumours he ran away. NHS was providing her with the basic treatment and they realise that her end is near so, she was sent to the hospice. She could hardly speak English. When she was asked 'what her funeral arrangement are' she went into pieces. I had a call from the community leader for a help as I can speak her language.

After making enquiries, what to do for a funeral if needed, I went to see her in the morning. She was in terrible state; scared, frightened and uncertain about what was going to happen. It looked that she had not had a change of clothes for days. She could hardly speak. Just kept crying all the time. She felt relieved because she can communicate in her mother tongue.

First thing, she said to me, was "would I be able to see my kids before I die?" Honestly, that broke my heart and I had to hide my emotions. Though, I was crying inside. "Of course, please do not worry, everything is going to be OK". I took some details from her; where she was living and where her kids were and who was her social worker etc. She did not even have the basic papers for her Id or her case with the Home Office.

I asked for a help from a community worker, whom I trust. I even asked my wife to go to the local supermarket to get some dresses and other basic necessities. Meanwhile I approached the head of the Social Services. She was horrified about the situation that she [patient] had not seen her children for that long. After few minutes. She rang back and assured me that the same afternoon; the foster family and children's headteacher will bring the children to the hospice to meet their mother. The words fail to explain the relief she had, when she heard the news.

Meanwhile, me and the community worker went to the address, where she lived prior to being admitted to the hospital. The Landlord was not helpful at all; he was not ready to provide us any access at all, but a cleaner heard us talking. She came out and said if we could come back in 20 minutes something would be arranged. We went back after 20 minutes; The Landlord had already left the property. The cleaner knew the Patient very well and she was sympathetic too and feeling sorry for the patient. She let us in and guided us to the dump and dark cellar where the patient's belongings were stored. Even though this landlord was receiving the rent from the home office; but the room had been let to someone else. We recovered some of the Bin-liners. We recovered her phone, files of documents and personal photographs and other things which we thought may be useful. The cleaner told us that the landlord was making her work for her keep even though he was getting money from the home office while she was sick. Some people do exploit these vulnerable people. That cleaner risked her job and provided us her number so that we could recover rest of her belongings.

I put enough credit in her phone, so that she could talk to her parents, family and friends. That evening her two beautiful kids arrived. There are no words to describe that moment. The joy of that meeting would melt anyone's heart. Their head teacher and foster parents of the children gave me all the details of her condition and circumstances.

Her condition was getting worse by the hour. Her tumours started to push forward which affected her eyesight. She was becoming more and more disoriented. Meanwhile there were management meeting after meeting to decide what to do with her case. I was getting more and more involved and my colleagues started to resent my involvement. She had started to cling to me for everything and I had to represent her everywhere. My enquiries were not going down well with my colleagues. I was going through some considerable pressure and I decided to do my best regardless of the consequences.

One morning, she asked me to do her a favour to send a parcel of her worn clothes to some witch-doctor in India who had promised her parents that 'she knows how to cure her for a fee'. I knew she was clinging to every hope she could find. I told her that I cannot do that but I recommend her to pray herself. She asked if she could do a communal prayer; which I agreed. I made an arrangement with a local Gurdwara [Sikh Temple]. I went on air on a local radio to appeal for general public to join in the prayers. She was weak and vulnerable. I had a permission from the medical staff for short release to attend the prayer.

People from all walks of life, faiths and communities turned up. She was aided to sit and everyone prayed from core of their heart. I had heard so many times 'when people pray for others the prayers often get answered'. Even before the prayers were completed the offers of help started to come from various professionals. Neurologist from a leading University left a text for me to contact him. A Barrister from Nottingham and many people offered funds if needed. I was overwhelmed with support.

The Neurologist took the details of the local consultant dealing with her case. The Barrister promised to go to the Home Office personally and appeal her case on compassionate grounds. Her treatment charged. Within two days she and her kids had a permission to stay in UK. Her status changed, she became entitled for all sort of benefits and treatments. Her conditions started to get better and better day by day. In a hospice there is average stay of ten days but she stayed there over ten weeks.

Things went better and better for her. Her brother and his family were granted permission to come to UK and look after the Children.

She had the latest scan few days ago and her doctor told her that all the tumours have disappeared and there are only scars. I met her consultant the other day, at the hospital, she said 'there is no logic or medical reasons for her recovery and she is going to write about it'.

Loss and Bereavement:

Death is identified as a loss in a society. Loss is different to everyone. It is unique to each individual. What actual happens; we regard that the immediate family is affected by a loss but in reality, it is far beyond an immediate family. My next-door lady passed away. She was living own her own for years. Her immediate family used to visit her on special occasions only. She had shared her ups and down with my family. We shared food, chatted about everything. She felt comfortable to talk to us openly and freely. We did the same. There was a unique bound between us and her. When she passed away it affected us more than her family.

Her Loss could be measured as a loss of:

Mother, daughter, sister, Auntie, niece, sister-in-law, daughter -in-law, Grandma, Great Grandma, even a Great, Great, Grandma and so on

Socially: Teacher, Organiser, Carer, Neighbour, Social worker, Religious leader, Religious preacher, Leader, Good Listener, Good Mother, Good Adviser, Professional, Reformer etc.

Good Story teller, Good Piano Player, Sensitive to other's needs, Good Manager, Good Colleague, Good Fund-raiser. Etc.

So, when we lose someone, one of the above is lost too

It is not only that human beings get effected. Pets also miss their master. Birds miss their food provider. Even the plants feel it, No body to water them and supply fertiliser etc.

How do we recognise, who been affected most? The spouse and the close family get the condolences and sympathy cards; do we acknowledge that it may be someone else needs attention as well.

When we face a loss of someone, we go through five different phases. The order of these may differ from one to another.

> **1. Denial:** Even though we witness ourselves or someone we trust gives the news but we still don't believe it. Our reactions are, 'It had not happened, it can't happen, it is not possible because I have spoken to him/her yesterday/ hours before, I seen him/her walking/ shopping. We keep doubting all the time.

- What if it is not true? How could be verified? We always forget that the difference between life and death is only a breath.

> **2. Anger:** We are angry about so many things, rather than accepting that the life is predetermined. We keep asking questions: 'Why it happened to me or us? Why didn't we try this or that? Why the doctors did not do this? Why the hospitals did not do this? Why didn't I go earlier? Why didn't I talk about this?

- Why people are intruding in our grief? We do not know

these people who are coming to us, why they mourn? Why people are giving us advice?

- It is so strange that how often we even criticise people crying, shouting being so quite when it is so natural. People get accused for play acting; 'look how she is crying her eyes out now, she always criticised her, argued with her, and gave her hard time, when she was alive'.

- We even moan about the timing of the death. Like the deceased could chose the time. Why it happened now? when I have this commitment on work or holiday or even a wedding or some other ceremony.

3. Bargaining: How often we experienced when the parents lose their child. We all feel it is out of turn. Even the parents often say. 'God should have taken me/us instead of him/her'. Death should have waited for this or that event. Deceased was more important than others. There should have been more advancement of medicine then we wouldn't have the loss.

4. Drawing a line: This is important part of a death. We want to witness or participate so that we can have a closure. Arranging a funeral, service, memorial or making arrangements for a legacy. By participating in a funeral, it reminds us that we are also waiting for this and a big reminder how to live our lives. By witnessing a funeral, it confirms that the body we used to hug, feel, touch, talk, see or recognise no longer with us. It has been disposed of. The soul had departed from the body. What happened to soul? It will always remain a mystery. It is a process of letting go. There isn't a doubt that we will face the body again. We may see images in our imagination

5. Acceptance: It is a long process. We never forget the loss. The grief stays with us all our life but we just learn to live with it. We get use to our new norm [normal] There is no time scale how long this process will take. Grief is personal. The things we took for granted, no longer there. We are missing all that. It is hard. Often when we talk to the bereaved and they tell us their experiences, life without your loved ones is so difficult. Some of them needs help and support. Loneliness, reaction of the society, family and friends is difficult to face. People do not know how you feel and what they should say to you. We heard people avoid the bereaved, even change side of the footpath. The spouses find it very hard to deal with. Their friends attitude changes, the couples they used to socialise before find it awkward to socialise when you are own your own. Difficult to cook for one. Dark, cold and quite home is not welcoming anymore. Lonely bedroom, cold bed, eating and relaxing alone is hard, Even going on holidays is difficult. One client put it so nicely, there is tax being own your own.

So eventually, we do accept our new Norm, but when, it always differs from one person to other.

Conference on What happens after Death

I just joined local Hospice as a volunteer. I was still learning what end of life care is. I had a call to attend a conference arranged by American Universities on behalf of end-of-life care providers, as a last-minute replacement due to an illness. I did not know what to expect and what I needed to do and there wasn't time to think either.

The conference was held in a stately home turned into a conference centre, with beautiful landscaped garden enclosed by a high stone wall. The approaching driveway was long and tree-lined, one side of it was deep blue water lake. First impression; what a peaceful, beautiful place to hold a conference on such a delicate subject.

After signing in; When I entered the conference hall. I was pleasantly surprised to find world famous VIP'S with their glamorous, colourful and splendid religious gowns and ornaments. Some of them had number of helping staff accompanying them. All the known faiths were represented by someone. The people you only see on TV or their pictures in newspapers. I felt, hugely humbled, honoured, privileged and excited. Some of them were, my role models.

The chair-lady opened the conference, with a precise opening address and pleaded to all the line-up of speakers to be punctual and adhere to the timetable. She expressed how important it is to learn their views, about this important subject, so that the end-of-life care-providers can do the right things at the right time.

Speakers brought their religious books to the podium with respect and some ceremony, for them to quote from these. Each of them, was greeted with loud applause. Once they started; they want to impress everyone with their vast knowledge on this subject quoting from their religious books to make their point and drive home that their views should be taken into consideration. Because all the speakers knew each other every so often the hall erupted in loud applause. When they were in full flow, nobody could dare to stop them or tell them the time is up. So, soon the time table went out of the window and the organisers have to accept the reality and everything started running late.

Speaker after speakers came and explained; how our deeds are recorded, how we have to face the special court, which will decide our fate either we will go to the heaven or to hell. Setting of the court was explained in every detail according to their beliefs. The procedures; how you will be brought to the court and who will be present. The special names like *'Jumdoot' [Court Ushers], Chitergupat [Court Clerk], Dharmaraj [Chief Justice], angels* were often mentioned. Other terms like *Judgement Day, Kiamat, Reckoning, Hisab- kitab, and lekha were referred to.* What was fascinating that every speaker was enforcing the similar theory.

Then came the description of the heaven. Most glamorous place one can ever imagine. The Magical Gardens with magical birds and animals. Magical foods, wines and delicacies. Glamorous people to serve, above all beautiful ladies for a company, which are only reserved for this place. Their beauty been described in detail. Number of these ladies you get depended on how good your deeds were. If you had made an ultimate sacrifice with your life for your faith or country you will be allocated with the highest number of these [*Hoors*]. The description of the furnishing of the places you will get allocated, the facilities you will have. The transport is described an exceptional. No taxes, no bills and no other expense, everything you can ever wish for, but free. No diseases, illnesses or discomforts. Always, you stay young and beautiful.

There was list of people who can recommend or fast track you to heaven. There was description of the deeds which will not take only you to Heaven, but your whole family and in some cases seven generations too. How the service of some individuals or cults or society can get you bonus points.

Then came a description of Hell. The picture painted of the hell was hard to listen to. The acts of torture, hardships and hard work could make any hard mind to cringe. How you get dragged into the court crying from beating. The tight little streets and the army of people inflicting all sorts of tortures on you that is even before you get the court. When you get to court, the court will order the daily doses of torture, according to the severity of the crime you have committed. You will be ordered to do a manual hard labour all day and night with very little rewards or benefits. The punishments were described. 'You will be thrown into a boiling cooking oil. Red hot pokers will be inserted into various parts of your body. You will have a bed of sharp nails. Your nails or skin will be pulled by pair of pliers. You will be put in front of hungry wild animals. Your food will be of live little crawling insects and only small portions to survive'.

Then came the acts which will end you in Hell. Adultery and prostitution came high up in punishments. There was a list of punishment matching to your crime. The description of the screams and sufferings was hard to listen to. There was also a list of people who can either recommend or save you from going to hell.

It was explained that the court's decision is always final and there is no appeal. Every speaker gone to great extend how their particular faith can guide you to the path of salvation, where you do not have to face neither Heaven nor Hell, how your soul can be immerged in to great soul God or Permatama. Even though details were fascinating, I started to get confused and bewildered by all that.

We should had finished by 5.30 pm, it was nearly seven and last speaker of the day was enjoying the applause so much that he wanted to carry on. The kitchen manager came and interrupted the proceedings to say the dinner would be served in 40 minutes. For me it was a moment of relief and to stretch my legs.

After dinner, most of the people started to mingle with each other as they knew each other before. For me, just few hellos and introductions I ventured out to enjoy the beautiful landscaped gardens; For me the gardens weren't less than what had been described earlier in Heaven. The tranquillity, smell, colour and the sound of the running water was really divine. I walked for a long while, then came to a corner where all the organisers were sitting and discussing the day. From their body language and their conversation, it was apparent that they were not happy the way the conference was going. They stopped for a moment and asked about me whether I was enjoying. I hesitated and then said, I am enjoying the company and the setting, but I am confused. 'What it got to do with your sponsors? How it will help them to better/develop/enhance their work'? The chairperson Jenny [not a real name] turned around and said 'that is exactly what we been discussing'. I said, 'I will not stop you then and wish you the best to find a way to put this right'. I carried on with my walking. It was turning dark and I thought it will be better to return to the reception and have a cup of coffee before retiring to bed.

Soon after the organiser's party returned to the reception as well. I thought Jenny took pity on me and said: 'you mind if I join you'?

"Not at all" I replied, 'It will be an honour to spend some time with you'

We ordered fresh cups of coffees. We had an open and frank exchange of views, about the events of the day. Very interesting lady, she listened very intently and gave me a space to express myself. I felt that we were enjoying the conversation immensely, before we knew it was quite late and we both acknowledged it was time to retire as there was going to be another full day.

I met Jenny again at breakfast, she was full of beans. She called her friend and said 'this is very interesting man, his, last night's conversation kept me awake all night'. Her friend wasn't going to let the moment go by, 'look, Jenny, tell me the truth was it his conversation or him kept you awake'? we all laughed. All day along whenever Jenny's friend Carol [not a real name] passed me, she teased me about Jenny and Jenny about me.

The second day started the same way and all the speakers followed the similar path. Nobody wanted to be out placed by the moment their reputation faith was at stake. Everyone illustrated good deeds and bad deeds and their outcome when we die. Each speaker was cheered by the others by louder and louder applause. I was getting more confused by the minute, during the cheers Jenny will glance at me cheekily, probably saying "here we go again".

We were running late; everybody was looking forward to the conclusions. All of a sudden Jenny called me on to the stage and said, 'please share with everyone what you were saying last night'. I was terrified; I had prepared nothing for this. I was shaking nervously, there were butterflies in my stomach. How to follow these world renown speakers and scholars. There speeches were full of references, beautiful language with immaculate vocabulary. Jenny noticed I was petrified, nothing to worry about, please give him a round of applause.

I walked to the podium nervous reck; somehow, I decided that I am not going to worry about my language, vocabulary or the people present but speak from my heart. What I was going to say was controversial and I did not know whether they will let me finish or boo me down. The only thing I was sure that my soul was encouraging me to speak.

"I have a great respect for everyone, who spoke before me with such a knowledge, wisdom and clarity but I am confused and looking for a guidance and help to clear my thoughts; I am sure that all of you will all try to help me understand what been said.

I am confused, after my death which court, I have to appear before. Is it decided by the faith I belong to or the region I have come from or the language I speak? I have issues with all these questions I speak a different language now, different to my mother-tongue; I was born in India but I lived longer here in England than that of my birth place; I do not follow my faith the way it is described by many of the scholars present. Are these courts are set nearby where you live? Or are these regional or there is only one supreme court? What is the waiting time? In what language they will conduct my case? Would I have a legal representation? According to what faith I will be judged? How long the case takes? According to what I heard from you, everything I did will be recorded and judged, please clarify whether every act will be debated or a clerk just turn up and declares 'his score is 49.99%' but I needed 50% for the Heaven; what happens then?

Even if it is decided that I will either go to Heaven or dreadful Hell. But I remember when I attend a dead person's funeral the body is disposed of often either by burial or cremation; on some places the body is put on top of the mountain so that the birds and animal could have their meal, some communities throw the body into the deep water so that the sea creatures could feast on. One way or the other body is not going with you.

Just suppose, one of you see me in one of these courts and suggest to the judge; 'I have too many marks for the Heaven, please give him that 00.01%' which I needed to secure a place in the Heaven. Please enlighten me, how will I eat all those beautiful and tasty foods when my mouth has already been cremated on earth. How could I smell and enjoy the described magical gardens when I have no body or nose which has already cremated. What will be the benefit of the company of the beautiful hoor/s [beautiful lady only exists in Heaven] if my body is not with me apart from huge frustration to both [Hoors and me] of us. While we are on the subject of hoor/s what could I do with 36 hoors for whom I sacrificed by body in the name of my faith or the country. It was really hard to deal with one on earth; I cannot imagine I am going to enjoy the experience of having 36. Is the Heaven being sexist place; what does a woman get when she goes to Heaven; 36 lovers or being a Hoor? Also, if you are a Gay what award you 'll get?

On the other hand, If I do not get a chance to see either of you in the court and the judge declares I am an honest judge and you have not made 50% so you have to go to hell. I will just laugh and say to the judge you forgot the people on earth cremated my body. I raise my left hand on top of a podium and smack it with my right hand really hard. 'Look, when my stupid right hand hit the left hand, I felt the pain and I screamed; which you all heard'. I remember in a hospital a Doctor gave me anaesthetic then cut my body opened and he and others worked on my body for several hours cutting here and there, inserting screws and nails, sewing with big needles when I came to senses I did not feel anything and remembered nothing apart from some bandages and smiles on all present there. One of them doctors proclaimed 'congratulation the operation is successful and you will have a full use of your arm now. Those hot cooking oils, red hot pokers and all the described beating will not make me suffer or cry out in pain because my body had been cremated.

I noticed, there was a pin drop silence and they were listening. It was comfort to know that nobody told me to stop or came forward to throw me out by then. I was encouraged to say more.

I said 'I want to share some of my experiences with you'. The other night my dear wife woke me up as she was restraining me and shouting "stop Tony! Why are you shouting? What is wrong?" when I got up, she told me that my body was wet with sweat and I was swinging my arms and legs around and shouting at top of my voice. I was having a nightmare. In a middle of a town, three men were trying to mug me and beat me up during the mugging and I was defending myself.

Then few days later, it was the same bed, same surrounding, similar climate, same bedding my wife woke me up "Tony, what's up? why are you laughing so much? What is going on?" Soon I got up, I protested 'you are a spoilsport. I was having such a good time with my mates whom I seen after such a long time, we were catching up. You have to spoil it; why couldn't you waited a bit longer'?

Please, trust me I do believe in good and bad deeds and also have a faith in that we are awarded for good deeds and punished for the bad deeds. It is like the dreams I just described before. I feel our soul always acknowledges when we do a good deed, it pats you on your back and encourages you. Same way when I do something not so good even though there is nobody around, my soul still tells me off like the time I went through the red lights. It really told me off: 'O' you stupid man, you could have killed yourself or some innocent person'. My deeds are analysed instantly by my soul. I face my own court all the time.

In my life, I have experienced both hell and heaven. I do not need to die to experience these. If you let me; I would like to share one occurrence with you.

I experienced the Hell:

'I was twelve and on the way to our school we used to go by a temple; one day the priest lost the morning offering; when he realised the loss, we were just going by the temple. He followed us to the school and complained to the headmaster. The headmaster summoned us in a morning assembly and asked which one of us stole the offering. In front of all the school and the priest, we told him that none of us had. But he did not believe us, he beaten us mercilessly with a stick till he got exhausted. The shame of being beaten in front of whole the school and the priest and having a knowledge that we had not done anything wrong was the experience of being in a hell'.

I experienced the hell:

'When I heard a news about my dear friend beer stabbed to death in a city centre full of people just for his phone'.

I experienced the hell when:

- I see on a TV or read in newspaper, when a young child of tender age, gets abused or sexually assaulted.
- Children starved to death due to the war or the bad management by the politicians.
- The hospitals get destroyed by bombs.
- People get tortured because of their opinions or they followed a different faith.
- Human beings destroy habitats for other creatures, damage environment and waste food.
- Armies degrade women as a war-tool by raping and torturing them.

I also have experienced a Heaven:

'I was three years old unaware that my dear mother was looking for me everywhere. I went out and started playing in a muddy pool with sticks near a bush in front of our home. Mud was all over me, unaware of the world, I was rather enjoying my unique game and singing at top of my voice. My mother feared that someone had kidnapped me or I came to some harm. She and others were exhausted searching for me for a long time; soon she heard my voice from the bush, she ran like an athlete and picked me up and hugged me tightly, kissed me all over. Even though mud had destroyed her dress and seeing a happiness and relief on her face...

I have experienced a heaven:

I was sixteen, working in our fields in a scorching heat 45c. My mum should have brought my lunch, by that time. Time was going by and hunger was getting unbearable due to heat and hard labour. I was unaware that my mum had to deal with a family emergency. Nearly two hours later my sister realised that nobody had taken my lunch to me.

She ran nearly two miles. Seeing somebody was bringing my lunch, was such a relief; I came near the water well and sat under a Mulberry Tree waiting. She was out of breath, running, she just passed a parcel.

Two left over Rotis [Chapattis] and small piece of mango pickle. I ate those quickly and drank the water from the water well while my dear sister sat near me. She was apologetic and explaining what had happened. The cold breeze and shade of a mulberry tree, with full stomach, I fell asleep.

My sister left, leaving me asleep.

That was the best mea and the best sleep I ever had.

I experienced a Heaven

When a client of mine shouted in a crowded market in London, "Tony, Tony". I turned around I saw a familiar face but could not remember him. "I am Mark [not a real name], this is my family" as soon as he spoke, I recognised him. He added, "I always wanted to show my family a man who had given me a hope to live when I was down and out" his voiced filled with emotion. I said, 'nothing like that I was just doing my duty'.

I have experienced a heaven;

I was baby-sitting my 3-yrs-old grandson. I had a heart-breaking news and I slumped into a nearby chair. My grandson noticed and felt alarmed.

'Grandad are you sad'?

'Yes, I am' I replied.

He ran to his toy's box and fetched a small toy, held my hand and said quietly in a soft voice

"I will make you happy"

I left the podium amidst a load applause, a world-famous VIP [my role model] walked towards me hugged and kissed my forehead.

Warm tears rolled down on my cheeks in an acknowledgement of a heavenly moment I was experiencing.

- Amarjit [Tony] Singh Bhaur -

I am extremely grateful...

...for the generous and kind donations made by my loyal friends and supporters, to make it possible to donate 500 Books to end-of-life care-providing institutes worldwide.

Mr Abdul Caratella	Mr Iqbal Johal
Mr Ade Johal	Mr Ishwar Rohit
Mr Avtar Singh Bains	Mr Jarnail Pabla Canada
Mr Ashok Jethwa	Mrs Kuljit Chera
Mr Baldeep Bhaur	Mr Khushwant Chera
Mr Balwant Bola Canada	Mrs Manjit Kaur Padda
Mrs Balwinder Ghathora	Mr Mandeep Bhaur
Ms Dalvir Kaur	Mrs Parmjit Pabla Canada
Mr Darshan Singh	Mr Sohan Singh Marwaha
Friends Motors	Mr Sarbjit Singh
Mrs Gurmit Kaur	Mr Subash Sahdev
Mr Gurnam Singh Grewal	Mrs Seema Sahdev
Mr Gurdeep Singh Chera Canada	Mr and Mrs Sandhu
Mrs Geeta Mistry	Mr Jeevan Gahunia
Ms Gurpreet Grewal	Mrs Joginder Bhaur
Mr Hamraj Kang of Kangs Solicitors	Mr Umesh Chauhan
Mrs Deepak Bagga	Mr Kulwant Bagga

If you either want to recommend an organisation or institution who will benefit from this book or want to donate towards this endeavour, please contact me.

I am looking forward to your honest feedback.

Tony Bhaur
amarjitbhaur@gmail.com

Available worldwide online and from all good bookstores

www.mtp.agency

www.facebook.com/mtp.agency

@mtp_agency

www.ingramcontent.com/pod-product-compliance
Lightning Source LLC
LaVergne TN
LVHW021657060526
838200LV00050B/2400